Who *Am* I?

What I Learned and How I Helped Other People Change Their Lives

ESTHER KESSLER

Published by:
Esther Kessler
AVENTURA, FLORIDA

ISBN-13: 978-0-578-92547-9

Editing:
Erica Rauzin

Typesetting and cover:
Gary A. Rosenberg
www.thebookcouple.com

Contents

VOLUME II: What I Learned

I dedicate my book to my Aunt Sophie (my mother's older sister), who nourished me both physically and emotionally. I was very fortunate to have two mothers growing up!

VOLUME I

Introduction

"I will be what I will be" means that I will enter history and transform it. God was telling Moses that there was no way he or anyone else could know in advance what God was about to do. He told him in general terms that He was about to rescue the Israelites from the hands of the Egyptians and bring them to a land flowing with milk and honey. But as for specifics, Moses and the people would know God not through His essence but through His acts. Therefore, the future tense is key here. They could not know Him until he acted. He would be a God of surprises. He would do things never seen before, create signs and wonders that would be spoken about for thousands of years. They would set in motion wave after wave of repercussions. People would learn that slavery is not an inevitable condition, that might is not right, that empires are not impregnable, and that a tiny people like the Israelites could do great things if they attached their destiny to heaven. But none of this could be predicted in advance. God was saying to Moses and to the people, You will have to trust Me. The destination to which I am calling you is just beyond the visible horizon."

—Rabbi Lord Jonathan Sacks

Moses was changing people's lives in the spirit of God. I am trying to reach for my higher self out of God's love for those I help, following the example of Moses who did what God told him to do. We all have this love inside ourselves. Through the power of love, every one of us can help change a person's life. God is love. As Rabbi Sacks wrote, "The spirit of God is available to all of us. It is up to the individual to become aware of His presence and choose to follow His will through the action we take. The bottom line is extending God's love through you. Everyone is capable. The choice is becoming aware of God within us."

This is what Judaism teaches. That's what religion is. As Jews we are the Chosen People because we are taught to act in the image of God. We learn to pray to God, to believe in the Almighty. We learn to become mature human beings, taking responsibility for our behavior. Only then, can we turn to our Higher Power, the God within us, the forgiving God, who teaches us to reach him in ourselves.

At a very early age, I knew I could change other people's lives for the better. I always knew I wanted to help change people's lives, those I love, those I know, like my mother's sister, my Aunt Sophie did. She changed me. She was my inspiration. She was my security, enabling me to grow emotionally. I was fortunate as a young child to experience such a person as my Aunt Sophie. I observed her caring and helping by listening to and loving her family and the people in her life.

I believe everyone can make a difference in another person's life. First you must care enough to help other people to make changes in something they are unable to do for themselves or where they do not think a change is possible. Sometimes, by example or suggestion, you can change another person's life.

When I got married and I had all my needs met financially, I believe that is when it began. As I changed my own life and grew spiritually and emotionally, I was also able to help the people in my life change for the better. I learned how to think positively, open doors, and find alternatives for an improved life.

I'm grateful for the important people in my life who helped me with my personal growth, including the teachers, psychologists, and rabbis I studied with, the lectures I had to attend through the years when I had the privilege of obtaining my undergraduate and graduate degrees. They helped me learn who I was—not who I thought I was, since I had a negative image of myself. I discovered that I am a worthwhile person!

I returned to college to finish my bachelor's degree while raising three school-age children. I am grateful to my late husband Alan Kessler that, fortunately, I didn't have to work, so I was able to obtain two degrees in the first 15 years of my marriage, and I could pursue my journey for personal growth. I am grateful to everyone I learned from, beginning with four years in therapy with Dr. Syril Marquit, and studying under significant family therapy professionals, including Virginia Satir, the author of my family therapy text; Dr. Harry Sloan, who taught psychosynthesis; and Sid Simon, who taught values clarification. I deeply appreciate the many teachers who taught me significant lessons, including all my professors at Florida International University.

Rabbi Herbert Baumgard of Temple Beth Am in Miami helped me nurture my family with Jewish teachings for 20 years. Alan and I were founders and officers of the Temple and part of its growth to 1,800 families. It was an active part of my children's growing up through their Bar and Bat Mitzvahs and confirmation. I studied Rabbi Harold Kushner, the author of several bestsellers. I learned also from Rabbi Kalman Packouz, who wrote the Aish Ha'Torah *Shabbat Shalom Fax* that I read weekly, and I'm learning today from Rabbi Menachem Smith at the Vi, in Aventura, Florida, where I live. I always remember something I learned about the Jewish religion: What makes us different that other religions? Judaism teaches the highest moral code from the Old Testament.

In this book, my goal is to share those values, my experiences, and the lessons I learned about life, personal growth, and spiritual growth.

I have learned that before you make your choices in life, you need to decide if each choice is good for you, and if so, do it. If it is not, don't do it. Consider whether it is a good idea, and then do it or not. This is how I have tried to live my life, and that's what I've been teaching my grandchildren, the ones who want to hear. The ones that I'm close to will listen.

ABOVE: The Pollack Family in Europe before World War I. *Standing*: unidentified sister, Bennie, two cousins. *Seated:* Ida, Zada, Helen, Natalie, Boris, and Sophie

LEFT: In Europe, seated: Ida and Boris; standing: Sophie

Esther and Zada

Sophie and Zada

Norman Schulman in Vilna
(Paternal grandfather)

Esther Schulman in Vilna
(Paternal grandmother)

Natalie Pollack
(Maternal grandmother)

Ida and Edward Schulman's wedding portrait

Esther as a child

Ida and Edward after they moved to Miami Beach in the 1930s

Esther and her brother Norman in the 1930s

Esther at the 12th Street beach, Miami Beach

The family in Ellenville, NY, in the Catskills where Edward worked each summer as a barber.

Esther in Flamingo Park

Esther at the Wilbur Apartments, 1944, about age 12

In the Catskills, 1947 (from left): Esther, Aunt Sophie, Uncle Louis, and Ida

Esther on Aunt Sophie Sprecher's front stoop in the Bronx, August, 1947

High school skip day from Miami Beach High in 1949, (l to r) Carol Shear (still a good friend), Stanley and Esther

Esther as a freshman at the University of Florida, 1950

Esther's high school graduation with Ida (right) and Edward, 1949

Esther's brother Norman, nicknamed "Truck," at the University of Florida

Aunt Sophie and Uncle Lou visiting Ida and Edward in Miami Beach, 1951

Esther and Alan at Norman's wedding, 1953

Esther and Alan's engagement

Esther and Alan's wedding at the Sherry Frontenac in Miami Beach. Left to right: Ida and Edward Schulman, the bride and groom, Aunt Sophie, Sharon and Norman Schulman

ABOVE: This hung in the Kesslers' home for many years

FACING PAGE: Esther and Alan's wedding

The Kessler's first house, 1444 Sienna in Coral Gables

Esther and Pam with
Susie on the way

We wish you all could see our new brother. Robert Hal arrived Thursday, August 20th, at 9:30 p.m. He weighed 9 lbs. and was 21½ inches long. Gee, he's cute!

Pam and Sue Kessler

Pam and Susie announce the arrival of their brother Robbie in 1959

All three kids at home in Coral Gables

The three kids

Three little dancers, early 1960s
Pam (top), Susie (bottom left), and Robbie

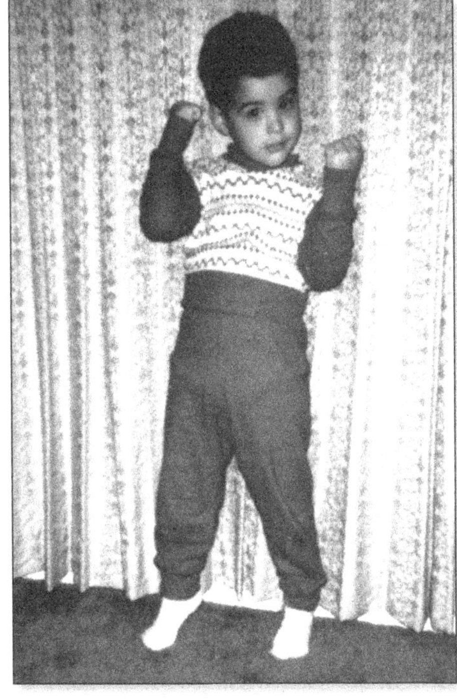

The three kids growing up

The Kessler's beloved dog Gigi

Pam's high school
sorority portrait

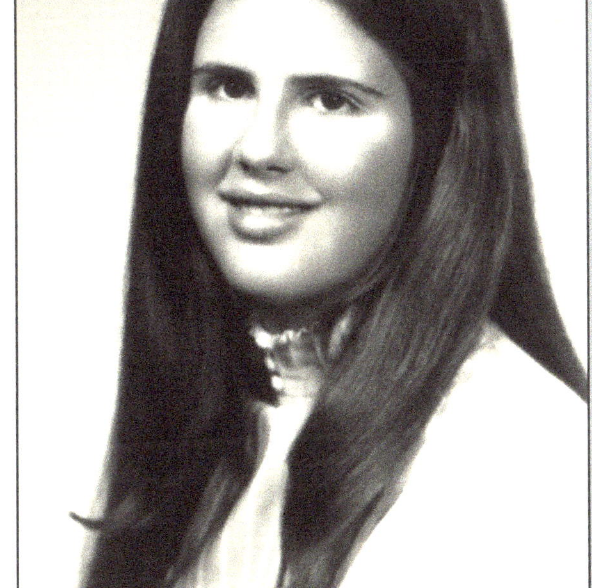

Susie's high school
sorority portrait

Esther and Alan at the Miami City Ballet in 1972

At an Israel Bonds dinner honoring Alan at the Fontainebleau Hotel

Esther, Aunt Sophie, Ida, and Edward at the Israel Bonds dinner

At a Temple Beth Am celebration

My Life Story—Part 1

From the Bronx to Coral Gables

I was born in the Bronx, New York, on June 20, 1931. My parents came to America from Europe when they were teenagers. They each had a long journey before they met in New York and married in 1928. Most of my life, I resented their European background and tried to Americanize them as much as I could, always urging my mother to speak English not Yiddish, her native tongue.

When I was two years old, my father had a barber shop on 174th in the Bronx. It was hard for him to make a living during the depression, so he decided to move the family to Miami Beach. One of his customers, a man named "Fat Harry," had a business driving people to Florida. He told my father in 1934 that Miami Beach needed barbers. My father got rid of his store and packed up my mother, me, and my brother Norman, who is two years older than me.

We drove to Miami Beach in Fat Harry's car. We had three days of driving, with my mother, father, my brother, and me, and some other people in the rear of the car. My parents kept Kosher, so I remember we had crackers, bread, and hard-boiled eggs. But most of all I remember sitting in the front seat on my father's lap and grabbing the shift of the car with my tiny hand. It stopped and jerked and went backward. The car had to be repaired, and I wasn't allowed to sit in the front seat anymore.

When we arrived in Miami Beach in 1933, I was three years old. My mother hardly spoke English, but my father got a job as a barber. Our first apartment was in South Beach. Then we had a bungalow on

Third Street and Meridian. Living in Miami Beach we would have hurricane warnings. When I was four, a hurricane flash-flooded the streets. In those days, there were no sewers. My father came to pick me up at kindergarten in a bathing suit and carried me home on his shoulders, passing through several feet of water to get to our bungalow.

When I was five, my parents put me in kindergarten at South Beach Elementary on Fifth Street and Alton Road. The school is no longer there, though a charter elementary school is in the same location. My brother was already in second grade.

While I was in that kindergarten, I had a terrible experience. One day I was walking home from school, and I saw three or four kids in my class coloring on the sidewalk in front of the school. I remember stopping and telling the kids you should not color on the sidewalk. They told me to go away. The very next day, my kindergarten teacher asked the whole class who would do such a terrible thing on a public street. No one answered. Then she said, "Well someone did it. Will anyone who saw who was coloring on the sidewalk raise your hand?"

I was very naive and always wanted to do the right thing. I raised my hand and told the class I was walking home when I saw four kids in my class coloring on the sidewalk. I told them not to do that, but they made me go away. I told the teacher who it was, but they all denied it and said it was me.

The teacher agreed with them and told the class I had to be punished. After school she would give me a brush and a pail of water to clean the sidewalk myself so she could make me an example. After school, all the kids passed by and laughed at me. It was a terrible experience for a five-year-old. I lost trust in all female teachers in elementary school. I think it was not until I had a male teacher in 4th grade that I opened up to learn. I never learned the basic spelling rules and the other things you are supposed to learn in early elementary, but I learned how a teacher's actions can affect a child's learning. I needed to share this, and I never have. I guess that's why I never wanted to be a teacher.

I remember pulling my mother's apron and telling her to speak English, not her native tongue, because all my friends' mothers spoke English. My mother was very Orthodox and Kosher. She kept a Kosher kitchen until the day she passed away, never veering, just doing what she had been taught in her childhood.

When I entered first grade, we moved to a second location, the Wilbur Apartments on Miami Beach, at Twelfth Street and Drexel Avenue, only two blocks away from three public schools, elementary, junior high, and high school. I attended Central Beach Elementary on Twelfth and Washington.

I grew up for the next ten years in that tiny efficiency apartment, four people and one bathroom. My parents had a murphy bed. I had the couch, and my brother slept on a cot in the kitchen. I didn't realize how poor we were. The apartment building had three floors. The neighbors became my extended family, since we had no family in Miami Beach except a first cousin of my mother's, Uncle Joe Pollack and his family, but they were grown-ups. They had a famous building company, Pollack Construction Company, and they built many of the apartment buildings on Miami Beach.

In the summer, my father had a job for three months in the Catskill Mountains in Ellenville, New York. Fat Jack, the driver, would take my family to live in the Catskills. I think we took that trip for four or five years back and forth. We would see my mother's family in New York during those years.

When my mother got sick, she couldn't travel any more. She had many years of illness. We had a Black woman who took care of my mother, my brother, and me. When the housekeeper left, I took care of my mother.

Why didn't my mother move from that efficiency? This was something I kept asking myself for those 10 miserable years. She always had excuses. Her sickness and having three schools so close that we had no transportation problems were the reasons that kept us from moving to a larger apartment. Years later, I analyzed the moving problem and finally realized why we stayed. My mother grew up for almost ten years of her childhood in a village in Siberia, where there were no schools. She lived in one room with her mother and four siblings with a big black stove to keep them warm and to cook their food. To my mother, this was beautiful, so why wasn't it good for her children? She didn't know any better. She felt comfortable there. She did the best she could. If she had known better, she would have done something about getting a better place for her family to live.

When I was 15, my mother's best friend told her that her husband's sister had purchased a duplex in southwest Miami (not on Miami Beach). They were going to rent the one-bedroom part of the duplex to our family. My brother had the rear porch. My parents had the bedroom. There was no air conditioning in those years, no TV, but this was one of the greatest times of my life. It was so clean. And I had my very first room by myself: The duplex had a front porch with windows that I slept in. My Aunt Sophie sent a bedspread and drapes in my favorite color, purple.

I commuted to Miami Beach to finish high school. I took a bus to downtown Miami and changed to a jitney to Miami Beach High School for the next two years. I graduated in 1949.

I was the first in my family to attend college. I applied and was accepted to the University of Florida in Gainesville. It was the first year that the school was co-ed. It had been a boys school previously. Before 1949. the University of Tallahassee was the girls' college in Florida. My dormitory at the University of Florida was brand new Yulee Hall. My class was the first one at the University with female students.

When I returned the second year, the weather was cold in Gainesville, and I needed winter clothes. But, instead, I had to leave the university. I wanted money from my father for the things I needed, and he told me to go to work. He said maybe you should come home, get a job, and earn money. That's exactly what I did.

I quit school and got a fulltime job at the First National Bank on Alton Road at Lincoln Road in Miami Beach. For the next two years year, I progressed very well at the bank. I got promoted to a higher paying job as the secretary of one of the bank officers.

I met my future husband, Alan Kessler, because of our move to 27th Avenue in southwest Miami. He lived in that neighborhood. I took the bus downtown from 27th Avenue, and one day, a handsome, tall young man was waiting for the same bus to downtown Miami. He was an attorney who lived on the opposite side of 27th Avenue. He introduced himself as Alan Kessler, a lawyer whose office was in the Seybold Building downtown. Once a week, he gave his mother his car, and he took the same bus I did. That's how I met him. He was the most eligible bachelor in Miami. He was almost seven years older than I was.

Several times we shared a seat on the bus. One day he asked me if he could borrow a cup of sugar one night. For our first date, he purchased tickets for a play at the University of Miami's Ring Theater. We dated for several months until one night at dinner at a restaurant on the 79th Street Causeway, he asked me to marry him.

We were married at the Sherry Frontenac on Collins Avenue on August 26, 1953. I had our first child, Pamela, in our second year of marriage. Our second daughter, Susan, was born two years later. Our son Robert, now Chayim, was born in 1959.

Alan was six and a half years older than I was. When we got married, he was a partner in the most successful Jewish law practice in Miami. His partner was Jerome Weinkle.

Jerry Weinkle's senior partner passed away the year Alan graduated from the University of Miami Law School. The story goes that Jerry went to the head of the law school and wanted to meet the smartest, most outstanding law school graduate that year. He met Alan who became his partner in Weinkle & Kessler. They practiced together for 40 years. Alan was exceptionally gifted and brilliant.

In the 1960s, we bought our first home. It was on Sienna in Coral Gables. This community was a great place to raise our children. Our home was behind the University of Miami, which was in walking distance. The children could walk to their music lessons at the University of Miami School of Music. They also had art lessons at the Lowe Art School at UM.

We had great events at that house. My parents were married 49 years, and I decided we needed to make a celebration. So we had an anniversary party, and my mother's two brothers came from New York, and I had all my friends, about 100 people. My husband owned the Dutch Inn, so we had caterers and everything we needed.

Temple Beth Am and Undergraduate Studies

Our house was also near Temple Beth Am, which we joined in about 1959, when the social hall was built. We were original members. Rabbi Herbert Baumgard was the original rabbi. I spent the next 25 years as a volunteer in the community and at Beth Am.

The first time I met personally with Rabbi Baumgard, I remember telling him that I was raised Orthodox, but now Alan and I had joined his temple, which was Reform. I told the Rabbi that I knew very little about Judaism because in my family, I was not allowed to question anything about religion. I never went to Hebrew school and because of my background, I always felt guilty questioning.

Rabbi Baumgard listened to my story and wisely told me that in Reform Judaism, it is a mitzvah to question! That moment took all my guilt away.

I turned to Temple Beth Am for all my religious education and a Jewish life for my family. Our children were very active in the synagogue. Pamela, Susie, and one of the teachers who was a synagogue member started the original singing group made up of junior high students from the synagogue. The teacher and founder was Harriet Potluck, the girls were both members from the beginning, and the group was called the Troubadours. They entertained at Temple functions and took bookings everywhere, even once a year at Disney World. All three of our children participated while they were growing up. As Pamela says, "We moved on after a few years, but the Troubadours endured for many years."

All three of my children were very musical even then. I gave them music lessons because I had never had that opportunity as a child. I'd always wanted music lessons, so I gave them to all my children, piano lessons, and guitar lessons. Studies say that playing music—and even hearing it—may improve memory, logic, and creativity. I believe that. After all, Pam became an incredible music teacher and so far has taught several hundred young students to read music.

Alan became the president of the shul. He was the president of every organization he ever joined. He spoke beautifully, and he was handsome and very bright. The Temple was just starting, so he joined the board and worked himself up to president, and the congregation grew to 1,800 families. Alan and I both attended many conventions of the Union of Reform Temples. I especially remember the first convention in Montreal, Canada. John F. Kennedy was killed on November 22, 1963, the same day we flew back to Miami.

I have a clipping from the Jewish Floridian newspaper dated Friday, June 9, 1967. It covers Temple Beth Am's installation dinner where, for the first time, a husband and wife—Alan and I—were named as president of the synagogue and president of the Sisterhood.

As a family, we enjoyed all that Temple Beth Am had to offer. Our three children, Pamela, Susie, and Robbie all attended Sunday school and Hebrew school. They were Bat and Bar Mitzvahed at the Temple and confirmed there. We were still in the Gables house for Robbie's Bar Mitzvah in 1972. His bar mitzvah was over the top. We had 200 people in the Grand Ballroom at the Eden Roc Hotel in Miami Beach. At the time, Alan was opening his Dutch Inn at Disney World, and he needed a manager. So they approached the manager of the Eden Roc and took the whole staff to the Dutch Inn in Orlando.

My children also attended Camp Coleman, the Union of American Hebrew Congregations camp in the north Georgia mountains each summer as campers and counselors. The kids always said the summers at Camp Coleman made their awareness of Judaism come together, that they learned more Judaism there than anywhere else. Robbie (Chayim) was the camp's song leader for two years.

I was a volunteer at the synagogue for 25 years while raising my family. At one point, the other temples in the Miami area were getting rid of their rabbis or changing to new ones. Our rabbi did not have a lifetime contract, and I felt he deserved one. He was our first and only rabbi. I felt he would be able to give our Temple so much more if he had a lifetime contract. I told my husband he needed to get Rabbi Baumgard a lifetime contract, and that he was the only one who could get it done, and he accomplished it!

The Rabbi wanted my husband to be honored for his outstanding work at the Temple at a special service at the Reform temple on Miami Beach. The three Reform temples in the area were honored. We attended the service. The first temple, Temple Israel, under Rabbi Joseph Narot, honored a husband and wife. The second temple, Beth Shalom, also honored a husband and wife. Its rabbi, Leon Kronish, used to say Beth Am was in the Negev because it was so far out of town. And then for our temple, Beth Am, Rabbi Baumgard called my husband up to the pulpit to be honored alone. I felt hurt, and I was crying as we drove home. I told him it was me who told him to work to get the rabbi his lifetime contract. I had worked as hard as any other person for more than 25 years.

My husband later made the rabbi aware of my constant urging him to obtain this security for him. When Rabbi Baumgard got his lifetime contract, he was able to create the Temple and accomplish all that he did for thousands of Jewish families in southern Dade Country. He started a reform Jewish day school, the first one in the United States. It was extremely successful, and all the money it made enabled the Temple to grow and thrive. Thousands of students' families had to join the Temple to go to the school. It has been established for more than 50 years now.

The same year as the Reform temple dinner, Beth Am's board chose Alan, who was president of the synagogue, to be the honoree at the Temple Beth Am Israel Bonds dinner for his outstanding work at the Temple. About 250 members of Beth Am came to an elaborate dinner at the Fontainebleau Hotel on Miami Beach.

Over the years when our children were growing up, our family helped make tremendous changes at Beth Am. I remember our big discussion as to whether our membership should remain open or should be closed. Alan led the Temple to remain open, a decision which had the greatest impact on its growth. It became the largest Reform congregation in the southern United States. He was also elected to the board of the Union of Reform Temples, where he served for more than ten years. We attended the Union's biennial meetings in major US and Canadian cities. Usually there would be more than 3,000 delegates.

Our first biennial was in Montreal. I was in my late 20s, and it was the first time I met Rabbi Baumgard on a personal level. I remember him asking me about my family background in Judaism. I told him my parents were Orthodox, but that I chose not to be. I felt very guilty about it. I explained that all during my childhood, I would question everything about religion and my Mother would never explain. I was told I was bad if I didn't follow her teachings. My Mother was taught, herself, never to question, and she blindly followed whatever her parents had done in Europe. Rabbi Baumgard then changed my life as far as my Jewishness was concerned by telling me that "to question is a mitzvah—good deed—in Reform Judaism." From that day on, I attended every class at Temple Beth Am, and I grew as a spiritual woman as I gained the knowledge to be proud of my heritage.

While I was on the Temple board, I also did other community volunteer work. For example, in 1972, I joined the founding board of the Miami City Ballet with my friend Wendy Rothfield. I especially remember the amazing masked ball we held that year to benefit the Miami City Ballet.

When I was president of the Sisterhood, there was a lot of fighting. One difficult discussion went on for several months. We used to buy Oneg Shabbat baked goods from Andalusia Bakery. Then a new sisterhood member joined the Temple. Her husband owned a bakery in South Miami, and she thought the Sisterhood should stop buying cakes from Andalusia and buy from him. Each meeting became a battleground about changing bakeries.

I decided to discuss the problem with Rabbi Baumgard. So, I made an appointment and told him the problem at the Sisterhood meeting.

He said, "Esther, have you tasted the pastry at the new bakery."

I told him, "Yes, I had."

He then asked me, "Which is better."

I thought for a minute, and I replied, "Andulusia is better."

The Rabbi immediately told me to keep Andalusia and not to change bakeries. I was curious why he made that decision so quickly, so I asked him. He explained that he wanted all the children of the members of the Temple to remember the delicious taste and pleasure they received after Friday night services at Beth Am for the rest of their lives!

Some 45 years later, I was telling this story and my son Chayim (Robert changed his name as an adult when he became Orthodox) agreed. He told me, "Mom, don't you remember. That's why I was so good on Friday night, if I was bad you wouldn't take me, and I loved that pastry. I couldn't get enough because they tasted so good. I couldn't wait to go to Temple on Friday nights."

While my children were in school and while I was a synagogue volunteer, I went to college for more than 10 years to earn my bachelors' degree. I was always going to classes and constantly trying to earn credits. I never gave up; neither did my mother, who never had the opportunity to learn to read and write. She went to Lindsay Hopkins vocational school as an adult to learn to be literate. She took a bus five days a week across to Miami to learn what she had missed in elementary school.

When I graduated from FIU in 1974, Alan and our children gave me a wonderful surprise party. I was so surprised and delighted. He sent out an invitation that said:

We're having a Senior Prom
For Esther, wife and mom.
The occasion is her college graduation,
And we are filled with admiration.
It's going to be a surprise for all.
Skits, dancing, food, and a ball.
RSVP as quick as can be,
And whatever you do, just tell me (Alan).

About 150 people came to the party, which was at the Coconut Grove Hotel. I have many pictures, and I remember my children singing to me:

What would we do if we didn't have Mom? How would we manage to get along?

Through your kindness and generosity, we now have a wonderful family.

(Chorus) Now you're graduating from FIU, and Mom we want to say, "We love you!

Off to school and out of the house, accomplishing things like Mighty Mouse,

Coming home to be with your spouse, who just spent the day with Mickey Mouse. (Chorus)

Then Susie sang:

All the goodness I've learned has come from you, giving of myself is what I've learned to do.

College is coming, so wait and see. I'll be the smartest of the family. (Chorus)

And Pam sang:

The oldest one is put to the test, striving to achieve all that is best,

The love and guidance you've given to me has set my paths to prosperity.

And Robbie sang:

What would I do if Mom wasn't there? How would I ever get anywhere?

Pretty soon you'll have me alone; how can you give me more love than you've already shown.

And together:

You've worked so hard to achieve this goal, and showed love and kindness throughout your role.

Now you're graduating from FIU, and Mom we want to say, "We love you!"

The *Miami Herald* ran a short story that said: "Esther Kessler graduated from Florida International University this week after a college break of 25 years, and for her and her family, there was a graduation party to end all graduation parties. Esther's husband Alan and their three children Susie, Pam, and Robbie, planned a surprise prom for her and about 150 guests at the Coconut Grove hotel. The dress was formal. Each lady received a corsage, and after a sit-down dinner the family entertained with skits and singing." Then the story listed so many of our dear friends who were there, including many of our friends from Temple Beth Am.

That same year, I started a singles group at the Temple, the first Jewish singles group in Miami. The churches were having singles groups, so I went to the rabbi and told him I thought our temple needed to start one. I had so many single friends, and I knew of lots of single Jewish men going to the church singles groups. When I started our group, there was a big article in *The Miami Herald*. It was very successful. We met once a week in the synagogue's large social hall, and we had music and refreshments. Many relationships and weddings happened through the years thanks to that group. (Little did I know I would join and run the meetings after Alan and I divorced in 1986.)

In time, I won election as the first woman Vice President of Temple Beth Am. It was a big thing in those days. No woman had ever even been considered before, and I won. Until then, the only board office women had held was recording secretary. A group of Temple Beth Am women got together to accomplish this great victory. In those days, women were not temple vice presidents. I broke the norm, I guess, and I even received a plaque.

However, I eventually decided not to continue to take leadership roles at the Temple. Over time, the politics got to be too much for me. And other women there were desperate to become president. They wanted it more than I did, so I made a big decision: I quit. I realized that synagogue politics was not where I chose to continue to put my time. Instead, I went back to college to earn my master's degree—and I never became the first woman president of Beth Am.

However, even after I was no longer vice president of the synagogue, it remained very important in our lives. Alan and I had joined the first chavurah at Beth Am some 25 years earlier, and we were always involved. Chavurah Achat had 12 couples, 24 people. We met one Sunday night every month. It kept me involved for 45 years. We did so many things all those years, though everything had to relate to Judaism. We had holidays with the kids, picnics, and even seder in Matheson Hammock park.

This was my extended family, all leaders from Beth Am. We met monthly for more than 40 years. The chavurah was significant in my life for all that time. The 12 couples were mostly board members and people who were involved in the Temple. Rabbi Baumgard and his wife and five former presidents and their wives were the original members. The Temple had become so big, it was difficult to get to know people. The chavurah was a close-knit, small group.

One month a year each couple had a turn to entertain, offer a program, and make dinner for the others. After several years, we decided that the only rule about the entertainment was that it had to be something Jewish. I believe that held our group together for all those years. (Alan and I divorced in 1986, and, in time, I would bring the man I was dating to chavurah. He was an atheist, but he loved going. He was raised Orthodox, and it brought back his family and his childhood.)

Our chavurah celebrated each Jewish holiday, bar and bat mitzvahs, engagements, and weddings. We were like an extended family. We formed lifelong relationships as wonderful friends. We celebrate simchas and had gift exchanges, fun, and games at Chanukah. I remember once when it was my turn to offer a program, I asked people to write about what chavurah meant to them. The responses were moving and eloquent.

The chavurah lasted until all the men died or people started moving north. As it wound down, we stopped cooking and went to restaurants. The sad ending of the chavurah is part of life's expectations. Through the years, we changed our meetings. As we grew older, driving at night became a problem, so we made it our meeting time Sunday brunch instead. We'd have the group meet at our favorite restaurants, and the host couple would pay for everyone.

As we aged, we would lose the husbands as they died, one by one, and we all comforted each other with each loss of a spouse. I continued with the chavurah for 20 years after Alan and I divorced in 1986. After 42 years of meeting, the group was down to five ladies, and each one moved away to be closer to her children or to enter assisted living. So the chavurah ended as many good things finally do. I miss those days and those gatherings, but I have wonderful memories.

I had enrolled in St. Thomas University in the early 1980s (after

Robbie left for Northwestern University). I finished my master's in psychology. I went to the university because I wanted knowledge. I became licensed as a family counselor and therapist, but I didn't have to work at the time, since Alan made a very good living. We had a beautiful six-bedroom home in Kendall on two acres with a pool and a tennis court. My close friends included my two weekly lunch and tennis partners, Marge Davis and Dallas Weinstein. We were together every week from 1980 to 1995.

We loved it when all of our children's friends congregated at our home. But still, I had a great feeling of achievement for a woman of 46, and I wanted to look for a job.

Fortunately, I able to find excellent work. My first job was at a nursing home. Later I worked with a Medicare health agency visiting patients in their homes and helping them with government community services. I also worked at the Jewish Vocational Services (part of the Greater Miami Jewish Federation) hiring nurses' aides to work in the homes of elderly patients. I hired the aides with green cards and placed them with elderly Jewish clients who called the JVS for services. The clients paid the aides directly. This was a service that Jewish Vocational Services started to help the elderly in the Jewish community in Miami and Miami Beach.

After Alan and I divorced in 1986, I had to leave my job because Jewish Vocational Services no longer could afford medical insurance for parttime staff members like me. That meant I had to get another job in order to obtain health insurance. I applied for work at a home health agency on US 1 in Miami. This was similar to my old job. I coordinated a meaningful program and served clients. We received a grant to train nurses' aides to help Alzheimer's patients and give respite to their caregivers. The government paid for the aides' salary. The grant was given to us to assess whether giving caregivers this kind of help would mean that patients wouldn't need hospital care and to test the costs. Years later, centers were opened to assist the care givers by providing places they could take their loved ones for several hours. The government paid the nursing homes and helped the caregivers with their health. The idea was to keep them from needing hospital care. Today, this is an ongoing program provided by Medicare for senior citizens throughout the United States.

I loved the job, and I was very into arranging care for people who truly needed it, Alzheimer's patients. I was making $45,000 a year, and I felt so capable.

But after a year there, I had a horrible car accident. That was in 1989, the year that Susie got married, Alan died, and we learned that Pamela had a brain tumor. She had brain surgery in Washington, DC, where she lived.

The night before my accident was a Friday. I met with an insurance guy who told me what I needed to buy in case something happened to me. He told me about disability insurance. What did I know about that? Alan had done everything along those lines. Instead of signing it, I took it home to study and think about. The next night, Saturday night, I had that accident.

I learned that "he who hesitates is lost." I had procrastinated on buying the insurance. That delay cost me $200,000. I didn't have anything from anybody. I didn't have disability insurance, because I had hesitated. Now I know if something is good to do, go ahead and do it. My husband was a lawyer, and he had taken care of all those things. I didn't know I could. I didn't know I was a worthwhile person. I thought the man had all the power. I didn't know that it was me all along.

In the accident, my face went through the car's windshield. I had to have plastic surgery and a hip replacement. I had to recuperate for two years before I could work again. Chayim (Robbie) even moved back to Miami to help care for me as I recovered. His two sisters were married, and living in other cities, and I needed him desperately.

In the meantime, I continued to live at Grove Isle, where I lived 13 years total. After the accident, I lost my job, and I dedicated myself to working and learning. It took me two years to walk again, so it was three years before I looked for another job. Meanwhile, I started going to workshops, and that led to more workshops. Then I found a part-time job helping the elderly residents of a low-cost housing building on Miami Beach.

We will come back to my story—my life after the accident and the people I was able to help and everything that I learned—but first, let me share some background about my family.

MY MOTHER'S FAMILY'S STORY

Aunt Sophie Sprecher

Aunt Sophie, my mother's sister, always took care of me. She was a mother-figure in my life. She had no children of her own. She made me feel secure and always met my needs, even long distance from New York to Florida during my childhood. Packages came with underwear, socks, and things I needed. But mostly I felt her unconditional love from our conversations on the telephone long distance each week.

Growing up, I had only a negative awareness of myself, like my mother, Ida. All her thoughts were negative. She was always feeling sick. As a child, I became the mother, always taking care of her. The only positive person in my life while I was growing up was my Aunt Sophie. The way she acted and behaved was my role model. She was strong and powerful. She had a job like a man and earned a living in the garment industry. She took care of her father and youngest sister, and paid the rent, and called her sister Ida—my mother—in Florida. She took responsibility of caring for my mother, too, and her children, sending me clothes and telling me what to do.

I spent summers with her in New York. She worked, and I lived with her for two months. She was my security, though she couldn't read or write. She never had an opportunity to go to school. She saw the positive parts of me, and she made me beautiful dresses. My first watch, my first evening gown, my bedspread for the first time I had my own room on that front porch at 16—she even paid for my wedding! And, she made me feel beautiful.

I found a quote in a book by Rabbi Harold Kushner that all a person needs is one person who believes in them. That can be the one adult who can change a young person's life. I remembered that quote for many years, because for me that person was my Aunt Sophie.

I remember her telling me about her sister's son, who was 14 years old. He wanted to have his nose fixed, so she offered to have it done. She heard him and sent the money for his nose job, and it changed his life for the better. His parents didn't understand or have the money to do it. After his nose job, he became a very confident young man.

One day my mother told that her sister was very upset because her son was quitting school and leaving the University. He was offered a job as a manager of a shoe store. I instinctively knew what I had to do to change his life. I knew that he must not quit college. I spoke to my husband Alan, who had a hotel in Washington, the Dutch Inn, Georgetown. He was leaving the next day to go to Washington on business. I asked him to call my aunt's son to arrange to meet him at the Georgetown hotel the next day for lunch.

I asked Alan if he could give my cousin a job at the hotel front desk with the same salary the shoe store had offered him, so he could work for Alan until he finished college. The rest is history. My cousin graduated from college and was offered a job immediately. Now he is in his 70s and has been financially successful. He and his exceptional wife have raised two special sons.

Aunt Sophie married in her late 40s to Uncle Lou Sprecher, who had lost his wife. She raised his two sons. They lived in a two-story, four-apartment building in the Bronx with the entire Sprecher family. There were the three brothers and one sister and their families. Sophie experienced all the children growing up and was part of all of their lives. She would always tell me stories of the families in New York and their children when she visited us in Florida for a month each winter.

After her husband died, Aunt Sophie moved to Miami to live with my parents. She came with three bank books that she wanted to transfer to three banks in Miami, and she wanted me to put my name on them as the beneficiary. I refused to do it because everyone would think I made her give it to me. I was still married to Allan, then, and I didn't need the money. I told her to take my mother—her sister—on the bus and get her to sign as the beneficiary.

Who knows what life has in store for us? Aunt Sophie was 67 when she moved to Miami. The second year that she was living with my mother, they received a phone call from New York that their brother Bennie had a stroke and heart attack and was dying. I had three young children, and my mother was always ill, so it fell to Aunt Sophie to go immediately to New York. I made the plane reservation and took Aunt Sophie to the airport.

I never saw her again—except briefly on her deathbed.

She had a stroke at her brother's funeral and was taken to the hospital. My Aunt Helen, my mother's youngest sister, called me and said Aunt Sophie was calling for me, and she was dying. I left immediately. When I arrived in New York, my cousin Philip picked me up and took me to the hospital where Aunt Sophie was waiting. I held her hand, and she felt me there. I spoke, and she called me "Babelah." She passed away several hours later.

I went home to my family in Miami, but I must tell a very important part of the story. The money my Aunt Sophie left my mother took care of her financially for the next 15 years my mother lived. Several years after Aunt Sophie passed away, I got a divorce from Alan, and I could no longer support my mother, but Aunt Sophie's money did! Aunt Sophie took care of my mother as she always had in her life. Even after death, she continued to care for her sister and all of us.

When I first was married, Aunt Sophie said to me that the world was changing so fast, it was going to be difficult to raise kids with the fast-moving society and drugs, and all. She was so wise and aware about the future of raising children. This was in the 1950s. She was always telling me stories of the families in New York and their children when she visited us in Florida each winter. She always knew how to help her husband's family and all the people she cared for. She saw the future so clearly. She always knew how to help all the people she cared for.

Sophie always mothered her siblings, including my mother. She was born in a village in Lithuania and never went to school. Her mother, my grandmother, had nine children. Their father, my Zada, my grandfather, went to the United States to make money so he could bring the rest of the family from Lithuania. The plan was for the mother and the other children to stay in their village, and he would work and send money. Zada took the four oldest children—their son Bennie and three sisters—to New York.

Then World War I broke out. My mother's mother, my grandmother, was left in Lithuania with the five youngest children. The oldest boy, Sam, was in the Russian Army, and my grandmother had three small girls and a little boy. However, the Russians made it impossible to stay in the village. When their village was attacked during a pogram, my grandmother and the youngest four children went on a cattle car to Siberia to escape. She managed to keep them all alive. Aunt Sophie was the oldest of the four; my mother, Ida, was second; then came Aunt Helen and then Uncle Boris. My mother was always inward, not outgoing. From when Aunt Sophie was eight or ten, she was like a mother to her siblings.

My grandmother sold linens in the streets in Siberia. In their village they had lived in, they used to manufacture embroidered dry goods, so she knew good stuff because she had sold it in Lithuania. So, she would buy dry goods and sell them and whatever else she could on the streets in Siberia. They were there seven years, and she kept four children alive. Boris, the youngest, was short, cute, and very verbal. He got attention from people passing by. Boris was very outgoing and would help his mother sell on the street. He was a great salesman. He became a super salesman and worked in sales until he died at age 89.

My mother was a gorgeous child. People would always stop and look at her, and they would notice my grandmother with four healthy, gorgeous children. They never went to school to learn to read or write in the seven years they were in Siberia.

Forty years later, my mother told me a story about what happened to her. She said to me, "Esther, I kept my face in the window in Siberia." I kept saying, "What are you talking about." And she said, "I never moved my face from the front window. Didn't I tell you what happened? Sophie would take care of us young children, but when my mother came home one day, Sophie told her that I was missing."

My grandmother went looking in everybody's window in their neighborhood in Siberia. She went down the streets looking for my mother. After many hours she saw my mother's face in the window. My mother said my grandmother banged on the door and shouted so someone would open it. The Russian who had taken my mother told her, "You have so many children. We have none. We will take care of her and give her everything she needs. We will raise her as our own."

The Russian people wanted to keep "the child," my mother! My grandmother didn't want to give up her child. Grandmother ran to the nearest police station and got the police to come to the Russian couple's house, and she got my mother, who actually was kidnapped. She took my mother home. My mother was such a beautiful child, but she was forever fearful and insecure. She was always inward, not outgoing. Aunt Sophie was like a mother to her and her other siblings until they came to America when my mother was 10 years old.

The family's story is miraculous. How they survived when the first world war broke out, and how they managed to come to New York and reunite with my grandfather, after eight years—how they reconnected as a family—was a miracle!

Many years later, Uncle Sam, the fifth child who'd been in the Russian army—came to my house when I was married and living in Coral

Gables, and he was visiting from New York. I had two kids by then. Uncle Sam told me stories about what happened: He was in the Russian army, in the Red Army, in Russia, and he also was in the White Army. He explained, "I went with which ever army was closest to the direction I wanted to go. I wanted to go home, to get my girlfriend from the village where we used to live, and to take her to America with me!" He actually did just that. He got her, and they came to the United States.

When my grandfather first went to New York before World War I, he took his oldest son, Bennie, and the three older daughters, and left Sam and the three younger sisters—Sophie, Helen and Ida, my mother—behind with his wife.

By the time my grandmother finally arrived in New York with her four youngest children, two of her older daughters were dead. The oldest sister, Rose, had married Jake Kaplan. She died giving birth to their son, Leo. The younger sister, Gussie, was living in her sister's home and taking care of her baby. Her father made her brother-in-law marry her. In Jewish tradition, a single woman could not live in the house of a single man, so they married. She had a child named Philip. But I was told that Gussie had been born with a heart ailment. She died when her son Philip was six. The family would say she died of heartbreak when Uncle Jake fell in love with his secretary.

The middle sister, Sarah, married and had her son Abbie. She died in childbirth with her second child, my cousin Libby. When Libby's mother died, her father's sister and grandmother raised her and Abbie. (Libby later married and had one son, Erwin Greenberg. Libby and her husband retired to Miami while I was still married, and then I finally had some of my family nearby.)

So when my grandmother, whom the family called Nechia, first came to New York, her two of her older daughters were dead, but she met her four grandchildren, Leo and Philip, and Abbie and Libby.

Several years later in New York, my mother, Ida, met my father, Edward Schulman. They were married in 1928, I believe, and my brother Norman was born in 1929. In 1930, my grandmother, who had gallbladder problems, died. She was only 54, but look what she lived through.

My mother went through a very hard time when her mother died. She was so depressed. She had a baby, my brother Norman, who was two years old, and she was pregnant with me. I was born in 1931. but my mother was unable to take care of me. That is why Aunt Sophie took care of me—and mothered me for the first years of my life.

Sophie and her siblings never went to school, and she didn't know how to read or write when she came to New York. She never had the opportunity to go to school. She knew how to sew and, as a teenager, she worked in the garment industry and managed to earn a man's salary during the depression years.

I was the only girl in my generation of the family, so I heard all the stories that Aunt Sophie told my mother Ida. My mother and Aunt Helen, the youngest sister, were taught by example. They helped others in the family, like their father, Zada, living his life totally Orthodox, being kind and helping others through the shul. Aunt Sophie was very spiritual, but she could not be Orthodox and still work to support the rest of the family. She had to work like a man to survive and pay the bills.

From my Aunt Sophie, I learned to listen and feel someone else's pain as she did very early in my life. This is the essence of my desire to write this book. When I married and became a mother, I was financially secure, and I was finally able to help others, including my family and friends. I feel everyone has the ability to walk in another person's shoes and reach out emotionally to change another person's life. If you consider what is going on in another person's life, you can make a difference.

I wrote this about my mother, from her perspective:

My name is Ida Pollack Schulman. I was the seventh in a family of nine children born in Russia. My childhood was one I do not like to recall. It was threatening and insecure. We were driven out of our home to Siberia because of the persecution of the Jews, the pogroms. My father and the other half of our family, my four oldest siblings, went to the United States just before the outbreak of World War I. The rest of our family, the youngest five children and my mother remained and went through the horrible parts of my childhood.

After World War I was over, we were united with my father. I finally arrived in New York when I was 13. Learning that my two oldest sisters were dead was a terrible shock. After eight years, only one sister, Gussie, and one brother, Bennie, remained.

Getting established and learning to adjust to a new country was difficult for me. Because I was a shy and retiring personality, I relied on one of my sisters who was two years older than me and on my mother. I was agreeable to anything they said.

I was the prettiest of my sisters and when I was 18, a very handsome young man moved into the apartment building in New York where we lived. He loved me very much, and I did anything he said. After my first son was born, I was very confused because I lost my mother. My sister Sophie helped me raise my two small children. When they were two and four years old, my husband decided to move his family to Miami Beach, Florida, because of the Depression. He heard he could make more money in Miami Beach, so we had to leave my family in New York. We began our lives in Miami Beach in 1933.

Even though I was a social worker and a counselor, I could never tell my mother what to do. She was always afraid I was going to put her in a nursing home. She was convinced that an HMO was the best thing to do. I said mother don't do it, you won't get the testing you need. So she did it. Then she got a Spanish doctor, and they couldn't understand each other. She was sick and in terrible pain. I can't stand this, she said, they don't help me. So I had her coverage changed back to Medicare. I always advise people, "Never give up your Medicare." In those years, HMOs didn't do testing. Good MDs find out what is wrong with someone by process of elimination, but HMOs don't. So people died. I believe Medicare has made people live longer.

MY FATHER'S FAMILY STORY

Now comes my father's side of the family. My dad, Edward Schulman, was outgoing, and he loved to talk to me when I was a kid. He loved to tell me stories about his family. That gave me so much love. He was born in Vilna, Poland, and lived there until World War 1 broke out.

My father's father, my grandfather Norman, had been married twice in Poland, so he had two families. His first wife had a son, Harry Schulman, and a daughter, before she died in the Holocaust. Then he married his second wife, my grandmother Esther. I'm named after her. My father Edward was a second son. He had a brother Chayim, who was two years older.

In the 1920s, the immigrant journey beckoned. My grandfather Norman took Harry, his first son, and left Poland and went to the New World, to Chicago before World War One. He left my grandmother Esther, in Poland with their two sons, my father, Edward, and my Uncle Chayim, who was two years older. My grandfather made arrangements for them to follow him to Chicago, but my father, Edward, got typhoid fever at age 12, before his bar mitzvah. My grandmother Esther took care of him, but she caught typhoid and died, leaving the two boys alone in Poland, while their father was in Chicago. Edward was 12, and Chayim was 14.

Chayim was two years older than my father, Edward, but he wasn't as wise and sharp. My father, who always felt responsible for him. My dad was educated in Vilna, Poland, the center of Jewish learning. He learned how to read and write Yiddish and Hebrew by the time he was 12 years old.

Their mother, my grandmother Esther, had two brothers. The youngest lived in Vilna, Poland, and the older lived in Providence, Rhode Island in the United States. The boys went to live with her younger brother in Poland. My father described this brother as dirty, with long hair, like a hippie. My dad said his uncle was very cruel and mean and used to beat them, so he decided to run away.

At age 12, he got on a cattle train and went to a seaport. He was a stowaway on a boat for 10 days. He didn't know where the boat was going, and he didn't have enough to eat. He hid without food or water. My mother use to say that's why he was always hungry. The boat landed in Buenos Aires, Argentina. He told me he walked the streets looking for food and a place to sleep. He found a barber shop and asked if he could sleep in the back room in exchange for cleaning up. Arrangements were made. He learned to speak perfect Spanish living in Argentina.

My father had the address of his father in Chicago, and also of his mother's brother in Rhode Island and of his own brother, Chayim, in Poland. My father lived in the back of the barber shop in Buenos Aires for four years, corresponding with his father, his uncle in Rhode Island, and Chayim, who remained in Poland with the bad uncle.

My father helped his brother get a passport and come to Buenos Aires. My father did the planning and paid for it, working as a barber. He wrote letters to everyone and made arrangements for Chayim to come to Buenos Aires. This was before the second World War.

Uncle Chayim arrived in Buenos Aires several years after my father. Before he arrived, my father decided to go to the United States to live with his mother's brother in Rhode Island

In 1920, while living in Argentina, my father learned—before Chayim arrived—that his father Norman had died in Chicago. The letter came from my father's half-brother, Harry Schulman, a bailiff in the courts in Chicago who did very well. (By the way I finally met

Harry when I was 16. His wife invited me to spend a month in Chicago with them.)

Fortunately, my father's uncle (his mother's brother) in Providence wrote a letter inviting him to come live with his family, since my father could no longer go to Chicago after his father died. His uncle got papers for my father, who came to Providence after going through Ellis Island. My father was 15 then, almost 16.

He was greeted when he arrived by his first cousin, Bill Tribiansky. He first met Bill when his ship landed at Ellis Island, and his uncle wasn't there to greet him. He had died. Bill's mother, my father's aunt, was pregnant when my father came to live with his uncle's family. She had a baby boy, David, and two years after my father arrived, she also died. Bill's older brother and sister worked and raised David, and neither of them ever married. In later years, the Tribiansky family changed their name to Troup in Providence. David eventually became a dentist.

When my father was 18, he moved to New York to make a new life. He got a room in an apartment house in the Bronx and a job as a barber. In that apartment house, he met my mother, Ida. She lived in the same building with her immigrant parents. She was 18 and beautiful, but she had never been to school and could not read or write. They fell in love and got married in 1928.

My father's brother, Chayim, could not get a passport to come to the United States under his own name, Schulman, so he got a passport in the last name of Galus. He came to New York as Chayim Galus. He kept that name, but for years my father used to say to him, "Change it back to Schulman." Chayim was afraid he would be deported if he changed his name.

Chayim married his wife, Florence, later in life, in New York, and they had only one son, Philip, who kept Galus as his name. Florence had no family, just one cousin. Uncle Chayim died when Philip was 16 years old, and Florence died eight months later. Philip was a young teenager and all by himself in New York. I said to my husband, Alan, that I had to go get him. He had to come live with us. I was in my late 20s, and we had two daughters.

We went to New York to get Philip to come live with us in Florida. I remember we stayed in the Astor Hotel in New York, and I got pregnant with my son that night. I brought Philip to live with us, and it changed his life. I purchased a plane ticket and made arrangements for him to come to Florida.

I had my son, Robert, our third child, who was named for Philip's father, my Uncle Chayim, Robert Chayim Kessler, and I needed Philip's room for the baby. He moved into a small apartment with my parents. He slept in the living room on a couch, and my parents took care of him for two years. He enrolled as a student at the University of Miami and took buses to UM. We paid for his schooling, and he got a job at the University of Miami Library for spending money.

When he graduated as a teacher, he told us he had applied for a job in Los Angeles and had been hired. He left at age 21. We kept in touch as he later left L.A. to continue his program to earn a master's degree in education at Hebrew University in Israel, where he got a scholarship.

Letters followed telling me about his future marriage to a girl from South America he met in Israel and later of the child they expected. His wife's parents were ill, and she needed to go back to Brazil. The next time I saw him, perhaps six years later, he was coming back to the United States with his wife and son to take a job with the US Health Department. They moved to Albany, New York, bought a home and, fortunately, took out an insurance policy with their mortgage that paid off the house if he died.

Four years later, he called and told me he had cancer. I arranged for his family to come to Florida and stay with us and have a holiday vacation for two weeks in our hotel in Disney World. That was the last time I saw him. Several months later, he passed away at 37 years old, leaving a son who was seven years old. I went to Albany for the funeral. His wife had a job and, thanks to her husband, Phillip, she could raise their son in a mortgage-free house.

Providence

For 40 or 50 years, my father could not afford to vacation or travel, so he never went back to Providence. One day my husband and I were on vacation, and we stopped for lunch in Providence, where my father's family had lived. I went to the telephone book and found Bill Troup and David Troup. I phoned and told Bill who I was, that I was Edward Schulman's daughter. He asked us where we were eating and told me it would take him 20 minutes, but he would meet us there. Eventually, he came to Miami, and he and my father were together again for about six years until my father died.

My husband and I had next door neighbors in Miami. The husband was a dentist who'd gone to Johns Hopkins Dental School. One night, we were having dinner with them. At dinner, I was telling my girlfriend how we'd met David, my father's cousin in Providence, RI. She looked at her husband and said, "Howard, isn't that David Troup, your roommate from Johns Hopkins?"

David was the baby my father's aunt had before she died. My friend and neighbor knew David's brother and sister, who raised him. In fact, my friend went to David's wedding in Providence, and David and his wife had come to Miami for their wedding. Small world!

Many years after my father died, I found some letters from him. He made a point of advising me to marry someone Jewish. He wrote, "I have read your letter and card for the night. What about that fellow you mentioned from Miami Beach? John. Is he Jewish? Please don't pick your boyfriends from another religion."

The Kessler's new home in Kendall, 1969

Esther and the kids in Kendall

The famous sawfish caught in the Everglades

In Everglades National Park with a smaller fish

Cousin Michael Abramson, his son Adam,
Adam's wife, Alison, and Michael's wife, Sherri

Ida and her two brothers, Bennie and Sam, who came from
New York to celebrate Ida and Edward's 50th anniversary

Pam's Bat Mitzvah. Left to right: Susie, Esther, Robbie, Alan, and Pam

Susie's Bat Mitzvah. Left to right: Pam, Robbie, Susie, Esther, and Alan

Robbie's Bar Mitzvah. Left to right: Alan, Susie, Robbie, Pam, and Esther

Rabbi Herbert Baumgard and Robbie at his Bar Mitzvah

Susie and Pam played guitar at Robbie's Bar Mitzvah

The Temple Beth Am "Troubadours" singing group with Pam and Susie

Alan and Esther celebrate their 25th anniversary at their home in Kendall. Left to right: Cousin Betty Eisenberg, Ida Schulman, Susie, cousin Rose Pollack, and Pam

OPPOSITE: Pam's wedding to Ira Brenner. Left to right: Susie, Esther, Pam, Ira, and Robbie

Susie and Esther at Susie's wedding

Susie and her husband, Hugh Beeler, after their wedding

Robbie's resume shot when he went
to California as an actor after he
graduated from Northwestern

Chayim's fiancé Michelle's wedding shower. Left to right: Michelle Greenberg, Shirley Kaplan (Philip's wife), Libby Greenberg, and Rose Pollack. Esther's Cuban cousins are in the back

Chayim and Michelle at their engagement party

Chayim and Michelle's wedding: Pam and Ira with their daughters, Nina and Tamara; Michelle; Chayim; and Esther

Chayim and Michelle at a Sheva Brucha with her father, Asher Greenberg

Edward Schulman at the family's Dutch Inn, Hendersonville, NC

The Dutch Inn
in Hendersonville

BELOW: We loved to travel and went to many wonderful places. For a time, Alan was in the hotel business, and the three children posed for a brochure for the Sheraton Indies Hotel, his franchise in the Florida Keys.

BEACH AREA

The Dutch Inn at Lake Buena Vista, Florida. This was Alan's first hotel and the first franchise Walt Disney granted for Disney World when it first opened, before it had Disney hotels.

The Kesslers at their condo in Aspen, Colorado

The Kessler children loved Camp Coleman in North Georgia. Here, Esther and her father, Edward Schulman, visit Susie at camp.

ABOVE: Esther in Rome   BELOW: Esther in Paris

ABOVE: Esther in Las Vegas

Esther in New England

The family's first trip to Israel in 1969.
Left to right: Alan, Susie, Pam, Esther, and Robbie

Robbie on a camel in Israel

The family in Greece: Pam, Susie, Robbie, Esther, Alan,
and Aunt Lillie Kimler

My Life Story—Part 2

VOYAGES

Thanks to our three children, Pamela, Susie, and Chayim, I have seven grandchildren and six great-grandchildren. My grandchildren are Pam's two daughters, Nina and Tamara; Susie's son Eric and her daughter Allison; and Chayim's sons, Chanan, Tuvia and Moshe. And I have two local great-grandchildren in Miami, Chanan and his wife Tova's daughter Mindy and their son Asher, and four great-grandchildren in Israel: Nina's children Aiden and Amiel, and Tamara's children, Rebeca (Rifka) and Abraham. Given age, distance, and coronavirus, I haven't seen my Israeli family in a long time—and I haven't even met some of my precious great-grandchildren—but I hope to see them soon.

My husband was a leader and a wonderful man most of the time. He and his law partner Jerry Weinkle accomplished enormous achievements. They were campaign managers for a new tax assessor for the city of Miami, and they won. Alan never lost a jury trial, and this was the first of his political wins.

His law firm worked with five main clients, in particular, to get the Everglades designated as a national park. They won the license to run the concession company in the park. Alan was president of the company. I remember he arranged for Leroy Collins, who was the governor of Florida at that time, to spend a weekend fishing and seeing the Everglades, including the Sea of Grass and all the park land had to offer. We needed the governor's support to obtain a new national park designation for the Everglades. Alan picked up Governor Collins at the airport, and they spent the weekend in the park. One of the five clients who was instrumental in achieving the goal of getting the park designated was naturalist John Pennekamp. Now a part of the park is named for him.

I remember a story about that weekend. On the way back from the Keys, Alan suggested to the Governor that they should stop at our house (since we lived in Coral Gables, which was on the way to the airport) to shower and change before he got on the airplane back to Tallahassee.

Alan and the Governor came in the front door of our home in Coral Gables on a Sunday afternoon. Alan introduced the Governor to me and also to my father and mother who were visiting and to our two little girls, who were then two and four years old.

Governor Collins showered and dressed. When he was saying goodbye to all of us, my Dad (who was very hard of hearing) suddenly shouted, "I think I know who you are. My God, you're the Governor!" I couldn't believe it. He hadn't heard Alan introduce him when they arrived. It was an embarrassment, but an unforgettable story!

Alan got the contract for a national park, and he became the president of the concession company for Everglades National Park Corporation. He was asked to tour all the national parks in the United States before he built the concessions in Homestead. Alan needed to become familiar with national parks all over our country before signing contracts for facilities at Everglades National Park.

Alan planned a three-and-a-half week trip to visit most of the national parks in 1958. He obtained reservations at all the parks we visited. We were met at each park by uniformed rangers. It was the most exciting thing that ever happened to me! We felt like royalty. My parents stayed at our home in Coral Gables with our live-in maid to care for our two small daughters. I invited my best friend and her husband to join us for the trip across country. We saw places I had never even dreamed about.

It was the most eye-opening thing that ever happened to me. I was

27, and I saw snow for the first time in my life. We toured the United States from Florida to California, going through the lower states, Texas, and New Mexico to California and then returning through the central part of the company down to Florida. We went to Carlsbad Caverns in New Mexico, then we went to the Grand Canyon, Brycc Canyon and Zion National Park in Utah. Bryce was the most amazing place I've ever seen. The wind blew, and the rock formations all looked like cathedrals. We went to California, Utah, Washington, Colorado, and Wyoming. We saw Yellowstone National Park, Yosemite National Park, the redwood forest, the Muir Woods, and then Rocky Mountain National Park in Colorado. We went so high up that I saw snow for the first time in my life. I jumped out of the car to touch it. Then in Washington State, we went to Glacier National Park, and in Wyoming, we went to Grand Tetons National Park.

I also remember the weekend when Alan and I invited two couples to join us for a fishing trip in Everglades National Park. It included a planned farewell dinner for the head park ranger, whose father had been the founder of the Boy Scouts of America.

Our group of three couples rented a large boat with a captain and a mate to go fishing

We planned to have lunch on the boat and return that evening for the special dinner for the head park ranger's retirement. About two hours after we left the dock, the boat broke down. The captain contacted the park office to arrange to have another boat come to take our party back to the dock. Meanwhile, he asked if anyone would like to have fishing rods while we waited for the other boat. Alan's friend Al had never fished before in his life. After he had been holding the fishing rod for more than an hour, suddenly the reel began to run. He could hardly hold the rod. The captain helped him, and at the side of the boat something appeared that was ten feet long, or longer. It was almost the size of the boat, and it almost turned the boat over.

The captain took a gaff and tried to grasp the fish that was pulling the line. The gaff was the size of a broom pole, and it split into two pieces while the line kept spinning out of the rod that was still attached to the fish. The new boat arrived, and the captain said there were two men on that boat, making seven men aboard and three women.

The captain ordered the three women to jump into the new boat. Meanwhile, the seven men took a new gaff to get the fish, which they thought was maybe 12 feet long, into the first boat, to bring it back to shore. The managed to bring the fish half into the broken-down boat, and the good boat pulled the old boat, the fish, and all of us back to the dock. The men played cards on top of the huge fish until we landed. We were only two hours out, but the weight of the two boats and the fish caused a drag, and it took six hours to arrive at the dock, finally.

We missed the dinner, but a reporter from the *Miami Herald* was doing a story about the famous ranger's retirement. A big crowd was waiting for us at the dock, and they heard the news about the unbelievable fish we caught, and that we were bringing it back for everyone to see. Everglades Park had a gorgeous dining room where the dinner was held. Alan got the scale to weigh the fish, but, of course, the scale couldn't go that high. It only went to 1,000 pounds. It was a *Sawfish.* The saw part of its mouth was 12 feet long. They cut the saw off and took a picture for the *Miami Herald.* Never before in the history of Miami was a fishing story on the front page!

This was the largest fish ever caught in North American waters. It made headlines as an *Associated Press* story all over the country. The best part of the story was Alan gave credit to his friend Al, who actually held onto the fishing rod for two hours. Alan was invited to speak at several Rod and Reel clubs in many cities about that catch, and he invited Al to go with him. He told me that his friend was speaking at one club and referred to the string (not the "line") on the fishing pole. Everyone laughed.

Other fishermen came to the park to fish at the same spot where Al caught that fish. In the years that followed, four other extremely large fish were caught there. It seemed as though it was a place where some of the oldest fish came to die. What a story!

Alan and Jerry also owned the hotel at Duck Key in Marathon, Florida. It was a Sheraton Indies House franchise. They ran it for several years. They had a great deal of property in the Keys at one time. They made and sold subdivisions. Jerry and Alan decided to go into the hotel business in the 1960s. They built the first Holiday Inn franchise in Miami on Brickell Avenue just before you reach the entrance to Key Biscayne and Crandon Park. It is still there more than 60 years later. That was Alan's first venture in the hotel business.

Alan changed the skyline of Miami for future generations. He changed the zoning of all of Brickell Avenue to commercial development from residential for our Holiday Inn. He and Jerry also built a Holiday Inn in Homestead. They were supposed to get the franchise for the Coral Gables Holiday Inn, and at the last minute someone outbid them.

I believe that made Alan and Jerry decide to stop practicing law and start their own chain of hotels, the Dutch Inns. Their first hotel was in Disney World in Orlando. Alan went to California and obtained the contract from Walt Disney himself! That was Alan's first big hotel. It was a 200-room hotel in Lake Buena Vista, close to the original park entrance. This was the first area of Disney World with hotels before Disney built its own hotels. Our former hotel is now called the Governors House. After we built it, we franchised hotels all over the country. We had hotels everywhere. We built hotels in Hendersonville, North Carolina; Monterey, California; Islip, New York; and more.

Our Disney hotel had its official opening in October 1971. Alan and I and our children and the Weinkles hosted a lavish opening holiday weekend, inviting more than 100 friends and family to come to our new hotel, the Dutch Inn in Orlando.

Over the years, we also had some wonderful vacations much farther afield than Orlando. When Robbie was an infant, Alan asked me what countries I wanted to see. I remember I said I wanted to go to Europe. His sister and her husband stayed with our children, with a maid, and I got to go to Europe for the first time. We took three weeks, and we went to England, France, the Scandinavian countries, and Vienna, Austria. I bought all my dishes in Copenhagen.

After that trip, Alan and I travelled extensive especially every summer. Once we went to Italy—Rome, Venice, and Florence—for two weeks. The kids used to go to summer camp, and that's when we went away. We went to a city in France called Eze, where you take a magical path up a brick road to a cactus garden. The cactus plants were shaped like bodies, and had white hair. The array of these plants was very dramatic, like a graveyard in a way. The son of the man who owned the Parrot Jungle sold us the property for our Kendall house, which we built. He had a house next door. He grew a cactus garden after he visited Eze as a child. The family had a collection of rare bromeliad plants all over their property. Mrs. Shear used to bring me baby plants, and that's how I got my hobby of growing bromeliads. When I moved to the Vi, I brought 40 plants, which are now on my apartment patio. I had to have a big patio to bring them.

We went to Spain on one trip. We went to the Costa del Sol, and toured the country. We also took many short trips to the Caribbean. We also frequently visited one of our hotels, the Dutch Inn in Puerto Rico, near the Sheraton on the beach.

Our dear friends Wendy and Ira Rothfield and Alan and I went to the Orient together for three weeks. It was a fabulous trip, an excursion Wendy found because she was a travel agent. We went to Hong Kong, Thailand, Taiwan, China, Singapore, and Japan. That's how I become close to Wendy, and that's how we bought the apartment in Aspen, Colorado. We went skiing several times, and then we decided to buy an apartment in Aspen. It was wonderful for the family.

One summer, our family visited New England and Maine, and we went to Arcadia National Park in Maine. Many summer vacations, we spent in the Great Smoky Mountain National Park in Hendersonville, North Carolina, where we had a Dutch Inn Hotel. Alan also had a Dutch Inn office in Los Angeles. When Robbie was eight years old and the girls were at camp, we took him to Hawaii, and visited the

Haleakala National Park on the big island. Robbie remembers the lava flow and the wind, which blew off his hat.

In 1969, when Robbie was 11, Susie was 14, and Pam was 16, we took our three children to Europe for a month. I wanted them to see the wonders of Europe that I had seen. We first went to England, then France, and then to Switzerland, where we rented a chalet for five days in Lucerne. The most exciting part was taking the Swiss train to the top of the mountain to go to the ice palace in Jungfraujoch.

My mother's best friend and mine was Lillie Kimler, who lived in the Wilbur Apartments with her family when I grew up there. I invited Aunt Lillie to join us to go to Greece and Israel. Greece had the most beautiful scenery; the blue water is incredible. We had a private guide in every country. We had wonderful experiences. It was amazing to be in Israel for the first time with my family. I took my family because I didn't want the kids to go to High School in Israel, where the students all moved to Israel. So I wanted to show them the country myself, but many of family members eventually moved to Israel anyway. I never dreamed that would happen to me.

I realize now that Alan wanted to see the world. He had an insatiable desire to travel, and I was fortunate to be his wife. We did it so young, before most of our contemporaries could afford to travel. I'm so glad I went when I was young and could do all those things.

I was already involved in life-long learning. When my father had passed away in the 1950s, we were living in the Gables, I attended a support class for people who were grieving. The teacher suggested that I take classes with Sid Simon on Values Clarification, since Dr. Simon was coming to Miami. It was a very enriching and powerful experience for me. I became a trainer and earned my certificate. I worked with him for 15 years.

That led me on a life-long path of learning and growth, which I will describe after I tell you about our wonderful family, our children, and our grandchildren.

Alan's Sister

I know I changed many lives as a social worker, but I didn't expect to change Alan's sister's life. When my sister-in-law was single, I asked one of my girlfriends if we could fix her up with the friend's younger brother. I had seen him—he was very good looking. She replied that her other brother was looking to meet someone and, she said, "He's the best." Of course, they have been married 50 years—three children and six grandchildren later. I made her wedding also! And I changed her life.

My Daughter Pamela Kessler Brenner

My oldest daughter was an honor student in high school and college. She was the sweetheart of two fraternities, president of her sorority, a champion tennis player, a gifted teacher, and a musician on piano and guitar. Pam is loving and reaching for her higher power. I gave Pam piano lessons at age five and a half. I took her for lessons weekly to an excellent teacher.

When she was 13, a very wise friend gave her a guitar for her Bat Mitzvah, since she had learned to read music. She became an excellent guitar player quickly. I took her each week to a guitar teacher until she was 16. She's an unbelievably talented girl. She and her sister Susie were among the original members of the Troubadours. Pam attended Sophie Newcomb college in New Orleans for two years and finished at the University of Miami, where she graduated. She was a beauty and was a Miami contestant in the Miss Teenage America pageant.

Pam is very loving. I thought she could go to law school, and she did become a legal secretary. Now she changes lives by teaching music. She became a music teacher, because teaching music to children is her passion. She taught in many schools as well as privately, and music was and still is her passion.

She taught piano, but she would also teach guitar lessons when someone requested the guitar. She changed the lives of so many children by teaching them to read music at a young age. She certainly left a significant mark on hundreds of children! I give myself some credit because I took Pam to music lessons every week religiously. That is how she grew up. She has a passion for music as her siblings do. Her life is giving back.

At 27, Pam was beautiful and single. The Rabbi asked her to run a singles group. It was called the Calabash Club, and she and Ira Brenner—who was a weatherman who had come to Miami to work at the US Weather Service—met there and ended up running it until their wedding.

Pam and Ira have two gorgeous daughters. The oldest is Nina, who gave me my first great-grandchildren, Aiden and Amiel. Her second daughter, Tamara, also has two children, Rebecca (Rifka) and Abraham.

When Ira was working for the US Weather Service, their family had to move around a lot. They lived in four cities in 25 years. While they were living in Maryland, the doctors discovered that Pam had a brain tumor that had to be removed. She had some minimal memory loss, but eventually regained all of her memory. She continued to teach, and she knows about the wonderful life she led growing up.

After Ira left the weather service, he joined Florida Power and Light, and they moved back to Florida, to Hollywood. I was so glad she came back home. I had remarried, and I was living in Boca Raton at the time. Pam got a job working for a local Orthodox Jewish elementary school in Miami running the music department. Then, seven years ago, Pam and Ira made Aliyah, and now they live in Israel.

Pam's Children

Pam's daughter Nina is my oldest grandchild, and she gave me my first great-grandchild, Aiden. She left college in her sophomore year. She was a single mother for seven years. During these years, I convinced her to return to school. She had taken out a student loan and could never pay it back. The interest and the loan needed to be paid so she could finish her college education. I paid off her loans to give her a second chance.

I encouraged her to move out on her own, and said I would help her. She found out that there was grant money for single mothers to go back to college. She applied and went to Broward Community College and finished the first two years. I was glad to continue to help her out.

Nina went on a Birthright trip and fell in love with Israel. She moved there eventually, continued school online and graduated with her undergraduate degree with a four point average. She majored in education for the disabled. Her specialty was teaching art to autistic children, enabling them to express themselves in art. These are children who couldn't express themselves any other way.

I remember asking her how she got the idea to teach art. She said, "My mother taught music at home all my life, and I decided I could do the same with art. I was better in art than music!" Nina excelled with so many autistic children. Teaching them, she made a living and raised her son alone in Israel.

She applied for grants to continue with a master's degree program. While she was still in graduate school, she started to give art lessons. She's almost finished with her master's degree on a special grant in this most important field, helping special needs children! She did it all on her own. I couldn't be prouder. Her plan is to go to work and earn a nice, comfortable salary for her son and herself. One of her teachers recommend her to teach students in a university-level program.

She remarried and had her second son, Amiel. She is an amazing young woman who created a successful business teaching art and holding painting parties. She has an ability to teach people of all ages who never thought they could draw or do anything. She is very well known in Israel, and she also teaches in America through Zoom.

Tamara also went on Birthright, and never came back home. She fell in love with Israel, and was the second one to make Aliyah. Once both daughters lived there, Pam and Ira also made Aliyah.

Tamara married a boy from Israel. I went to the wedding, an Orthodox wedding. After her divorce, she stayed in Israel trying to find herself and her future. She remarried, and now she has two beautiful children, Rifka and Abraham. They all live in Israel. She is a very spiritual woman and lives in Jerusalem. She wrote a genius paper about the meaning of life for professor Jaymes Buick at the University of Tampa when she was only 19 or 20:

> *"What is the meaning of life?" Most human beings ponder such an inquiry at some point in their existence. Philosophically speaking, when a person stops and asks himself this question, he is no longer continually "becoming." Instead, existence stops and a state of meditation begins.*
>
> *During this meditation, people contemplate the problem of faith and reason.*
>
> *Faith and reason are both sources of influence that sway our values and standards.*
>
> *Reason is recognized as the theoretical basis of practical analysis and is based on procedural inquiries and proof. It conveys a type of certainty through demonstration, whether logical, ethical, visual, or spiritual. Once a notion has been rationally demonstrated, it is then confirmed as true.*
>
> *Faith cannot be demonstrated by reason. Faith is non-rational and cognitive. It's about a concept of knowing or believing in the unknown. The unknown cannot be justified by reason and, therefore, reason cannot advance beyond it. Thus, faith suggests that a belief does not have to be proven in order to be true. So, when asked what the meaning of life is, an individual's response could depend on his or her response to the problem of faith and reason.*
>
> *If a person is more influenced by reason, he may be more likely to*

view the meaning of life with a more rational, general understanding. Reason is the connection between the general and the particular. The reasonable person examines and analyzes details until he can demonstrate a general conclusion. A person meditating life with this perspective may focus more on all of life's details, occurrences, and events, rather than focusing on their overall existence. One who looks toward reason may find it harder to accept the unknown. In addition he may find himself continually trying to find proof or reasons for everything in life, and may be more agitated if he comes across something that is hard to rationalize.

An individual who is more influenced by faith may find it easier to accept that the meaning of life might not be meant to be fully comprehended. He is most likely not looking for a reason or proof of his existence. When faith is involved, there is usually a belief in a higher power beyond us, one that cannot be demonstrated by reason. With that said, a person who is influenced by faith might view the meaning of life in a more non-rational way. For instance, he exists and just takes life as it comes. Because of his faith, he may allow himself to accept that there may be an unknown reason for such events, obstacles, objects, and people being placed into his existence. However, he does not strive to find that proof of reasoning. When asking oneself about the meaning of life, a person influenced by faith may believe that there is a meaning, but he may just as well be content not knowing it.

My Daughter Susan Kessler Beeler

My second daughter, Susie Beeler, my middle child, was a teacher in Atlanta. At 32, she married Hugh Beeler. They have been married for more than 31 years, and they have two children, Allison and Eric.

Susie left Miami at age 18 to go to college in Atlanta. Susie got her undergraduate degree in elementary education from Oglethorpe in 1978. She started the first women's tennis team at Oglethorpe, and it still exists today. She also got her graduate degree from Georgia State University in 1985 in Middle School Education specializing in math and science. She became a fabulous teacher. One of her professors at Oglethorpe was so taken by her that she brought her teacher home to visit us. Susie had a fulltime position to teach in Atlanta before she graduated from Oglethorpe.

All of Susie's students in elementary school reached the highest level in reading because she had faith in them.

Susie taught school for fourteen years. She was very respected for her love and devotion to her students. She has always been a super teacher. Susie was in charge of all school activities. She wrote the curriculum for the outdoor education program for three hundred plus students. She handled student patrols and student council for the school. She stopped teaching for five years to start a family of her own with her husband Hugh.

Hugh worked for Delta Air Lines for 25 years in the Facilities Division. When he left Delta, he was responsible for the facilities operations for Delta in five major cities. In 1999, Susie and her husband Hugh started and operated a HVAC business for 20 plus years. Hugh ran the mechanical side, and Susie ran the business side. Susie had learned a lot about business operation from her father. Hugh and Susie worked extremely hard side by side for these years. Working with your spouse can be very stressful on your marriage. Hugh wrote this to Susie during these trying times:

My Wife, my Lover, my Friend

I loved you when the sun set yesterday, I love you when the moon comes tonight, and I will love you when the sun rises tomorrow.

I like all the ways that we hang out together, even when we're mad, and I like the things that are not appropriate for writing on this note.

True love is difficult to find, great to have, easy to lose, but hard to forget. I love you forever.

During this time, they also raised two exceptional children. Both children earned full scholarships to college.

Susie has returned to her love of teaching and success with students in the last few years. She has been working as a tutor for the last five years. Her students have been blessed to have her. She has been very successful in educating students, and that success continues in her mid-sixties.

Susie's Children

Susie's second child, Eric is a remarkable young man. He was named after my father, Edward. Eric graduated from high school in 2013. His school had 560 seniors. He was senior class president, and he was voted the outstanding student in all Atlanta area high schools and also in the state of Georgia. He received a week in Washington from the William Randolph Hearst Endowment which selects two students from each state. He had a trip and airfare to Washington to attend sessions of the House and Senate and also a meeting with President Barrack Obama.

Eric spent his junior-year summer in China, leaving in August 2013. He won a government grant from the U.S. State Department for $45,000 to live with a Chinese family for six weeks, and ended up living with two families in China. People pay $15,000 for their child to experience what he earned. He took his senior year over in a Chinese high school, studying in Chinese. He took chemistry in Chinese, received excellent grades, and became fluent in the Mandarin language.

Eric was always a high achiever. He got accepted to George Washington University on a full scholarship. He applied for the very prestigious Ronald Reagan Scholarship from the State Department. It had 130,000 applicants, and he won $40,000. He went to California to receive the award. He also won the $20,000 Coca-Cola scholarship to go to George Washington, which costs $75,000 a year! The college held his scholarship for him, a Coca-Cola scholarship, until he returned from China. The Reagan Scholarship fund also held his money for him until his sophomore year.

He returned to the United States after a year in China, and went to Washington to go to GW University. He took a master course in Mandarin to keep his language skills. There was an Ivy League contest in which students had to give a five-minute speech in Chinese. He won that contest and received a trip back to China.

There is always a reason for the things that happen, though we may not know the reason at the time. Goldman Sachs took Eric to New York as a summer intern. He earned $15,000 for two months. There were 40,000 applicants. He got accepted and worked for them for three summers. After he graduated, he got a full time job with Goldman Sachs on Wall Street. He lived on Wall Street for a year. Then Goldman had an opening in Dubai, he requested it, and they gave it to him. He has been in Dubai for two years. He was working at home because of the Covid-19 pandemic, but now he's back at work. He's a very special grandson to achieve all this and, as I write this, he's only 26!

I feel Eric is a future leader of the United States. His goal is to be an international lawyer. I see him as a future senator and leader in the future. Who knows how high his achievements will be. I pray that whatever he chooses, he will continue to achieve and God will keep him in good health on his journey in life.

When he was a junior in high school, he asked me if I would take him on a trip when he graduated from high school. I was so flattered and extremely happy to accept his request. Eric had never been out of Atlanta at the time. In the following three years, this remarkable young man went to New York for the Model UN Convention for his school and received first prize. He also went to Boston to Harvard University with the Model UN, where he also received first prize (a gavel from Harvard). Then he went to China for six weeks and to California for the Reagan scholarship.

The summer Eric graduated from high school and his sister Ali graduated from college, I took them on a cruise to Alaska, which turned out to be a magical trip.

Allison is three years older than Eric. I encouraged her to pay tennis at a very early age, four years old, in nursery school. Ali also played baseball and soccer and did gymnastics. At that point, her wise mother said she had to choose one sport and try to excel at it. Ali started playing competitive tennis at age seven. When Ali started high school, she was in the top 200 in the nation in tennis.

My daughter Susie had played tennis growing up, and she was on her high school and college teams. We had a tennis court at our house where Susie grew up. She gave tennis lessons to earn money every summer throughout her college years. Susie was very knowledgeable about tennis and tennis tournaments. Ali became an outstanding tennis player with her parents' help.

She was #1 on her high school team and also the captain. She received a full college scholarship for tennis and a free college education. Ali broke records as captain of her college tennis team at the University of South Carolina. The team made it to the semi-finals of their division. This was the first time they had ever made it to division playoffs. She graduated with a degree in business.

Ali has become very successful in the corporate world. She hires and trains people for positions in her company. I love her, and wish her great joy in the future.

Tennis was also a big part of my life. I had a lunch bunch that met every Friday for 20 years, a wonderful group, with Marge Davis and Dallas Weinstein. We would play doubles tennis in the morning, often with a guest fourth, and then have lunch together. Then the three of us would go for lunch to restaurants that were too expensive in the evening. Every week we picked a different place. We had a very close relationship. I never had a sister, and these were people who knew how to be sisters. I always chose my friends like that. I still do it.

All my life I had only Jewish friends until I went back to school. Then, through my studies, I met my closest friends, Gwen Randle, a school psychologist, and Vickie Johnson, a therapist. They have been my soul sisters for 50 years. We all got divorced about the same time, and we were starting over again together. We became a support system for one another. We have always been there for each other.

My Son Chayim Kessler

Chayim is now a CPA in Miami. He went to Ransom private school, and he was an honor student, but he never knew what he wanted to do. He loved music. He's always been active in singing. He's a gifted singer and very handsome. He got into every college he applied to, and went to Northwestern University in Chicago to study drama and music. He graduated with a 3.7 average. Then he went to California to study music and drama for seven years because he wanted to be an actor. I just almost died for seven years. His father was a lawyer, an outstanding graduate of the University of Miami Law School.

Chayim (who was called Robert then) was the song leader at Temple Beth Am. He would take the Hebrew music and give it a beat. When he moved to Los Angeles, all the temples there grabbed him to do religious school music, and that's how he made a living—he waited tables, he was a bouncer, and then he taught music and Sunday School.

He got bit parts and paid his rent and food by being a waiter during the week, and teaching religious school at the temple in Hollywood. He also taught music at synagogues in Los Angeles, playing his guitar. But for that work, he needed to know more Hebrew. He studied at Aish HaTorah, a large yeshiva, and became Orthodox in California.

Robbie called me from California and told me he had changed his name legally to Chayim Kessler (no more Robert Kessler). The judge was Jewish, he told me that the judge said to my son, "I have had a lot of people change from Chayim to Robert, but never Robert to Chayim." He chose to use his Hebrew name, which I had given him in honor of my father's brother. He decided to be an Orthodox Jew, and he and his wife Michelle raised their three sons in Orthodox schools.

My mother was Orthodox. Our temple, Beth Am, is Reform. Alan and I raised our children as Reform Jews. I guess I was a rebel because I didn't want to raise my family Orthodox. I didn't have a kosher home, but I was and am still a very spiritual woman. However, my eldest daughter and my son chose to become Orthodox Jews years later, as adults. Chayim became Orthodox when he married, and Pam and Ira made the change when their children were on their own. Now they live in Israel.

When Chayim had been out in California for three or four years, I begged him to come back and go to law school, and I said I would pay for it. I never stopped encouraging him to return to college and get a profession. In fact, I asked him if I could register him for law school at the University of Miami. In those years, there was a waiting list for acceptance. I called often to see where he was on this list, finally the receptionist said that Donna Shalala—the head of the law school, who became Secretary of Health and Human Services and a member of Congress—wanted to talk to me.

She asked if I knew how many times I had called to ask my son's position in line: eleven times. And she asked if I knew how many times he had called. Then she said, "He's never called, so do you think he really wants to go to law school?" Then he got involved with Aish HaTorah, and that was the end of law school.

Then came 1989 and my terrible automobile accident when I went through the windshield. I was alone. My daughters were married, and Alan had died, so I asked Chayim to help me. That's when he moved back to Miami. I was so grateful. But that's also how he met his wife Michelle. She was becoming Orthodox and was studying to become more Orthodox. One of the rabbis she was studying with had a get-together for young people at his house. So, Michelle went with a group, and Chayim was singing to entertain the group. When he finished, people were clapping. She kept clapping when everyone else sat down. She never sat down, so that's how he met Michelle. They now have been married almost 30 years.

Michelle is a Holocaust survivor's child. Her father was in Buchenwald for five years with his two brothers, and they all survived. Her father, my son's father-in-law, was a shining example of a beautiful human being. He lived with my son and his family for 11 years. His daughter never put him in a nursing home. She and her brother took care of him at my son and daughter-in-law's home while they raised three sons, my most special grandsons.

Michelle's father had no anger; he was all gratitude. He never talked about the Holocaust in the 11 years I knew him. He just said one thing to me, "The way we survived is that we were three brothers who took care of each other. If one of us got sick, the others stole food for him."

Now Chayim has his own acounting practice. He has a passion for music. He's very talented and volunteers to entertain frequently at local shuls. I encouraged each of his three sons to learn music, buying each one an instrument. The oldest, Chanan, was interested in clarinet; Tuvia played the drums extremely well; and Moshie, the youngest of my grandchildren, became a talented guitarist. He gives guitar lessons, and he's really good. So at least one grandchild has a love of music!

Chayim wrote two songs for me in recent years. His lyrics use some of my expressions. He wrote, "I wrote this for my Mom. I used some of her expressions…with lots of love. Kindness is her mission, and she should continue to spread it till 120 years."

A Smile Beneath the Mask

I wrote you a song, a little bit about a husband and wife. Sometimes communication solves problems.

You may not have noticed when you were rushing off,
When the kids were crying for you, and your patience was
  running short.
Your face was covered over, but our eyes were engaged,

And you didn't see me smiling at you when you went on
your way.
It seems I didn't care much as we were working throughout
the day,
But when your mask fell to your shoulder, and you began to say,
I should order out for supper, get Chinese and Diet Coke,
Your teeth were shining brightly—that is when I spoke:
There's a smile beneath the mask,
You don't even have to ask.
A smile beneath the mask,
Our love was meant to last.
A smile beneath the mask,
My cheekbones are rising fast –
And if you look real closely,
You'll see a smile beneath the mask.
It's been so many years, you'd think I'd have a frown,
Despite some lost dreams and things to bring me down,
Yet deep down inside me, there's a smile in my heart,
That keeps me always loving you like I did from the start.
I'd hate to go through life not being grateful for my lot,
Not knowing how to show it, not being happy with what
I've got,
So if you stand right next to me—even six feet apart –
When you look real closely, you'll see I'm smiling from my
heart.
There's a smile beneath the mask,
You don't even have to ask.
A smile beneath the mask,
Our love was meant to last.
A smile beneath the mask,
My cheekbones are rising fast.
And if you look real closely,
You'll see a smile beneath the mask.

Kindness Is Contagious

The more kindness you spread, the more kindness spreads around the world.

Sing it out, sing it strong,
There's nothing wrong with your unique song.
Kindness is contagious.
Kindness is contagious.
Kindness is contagious,
And that's alright.
Kindness is you; you are so kind.
You make the world shine,
And you're alright.
Sing it out, sing it strong,
There's nothing wrong with your unique song.
Don't say no, just cause they said so,
Better just to help them out.
Deep in their hearts,
they'll find where kindness starts.
If you make a kindness link between them, too,
I'm sure you'll get together.
They will sing with you.
Sing it out, sing it strong,
There's nothing wrong with your unique song.
Kindness is contagious.
Kindness is contagious.
Kindness is contagious,
And that's alright.
Kindness is you.

Credits: Words and Music with Registered U.S. copyright by Chayim Kessler 2020, Licensed by Hashbrown Music Publishing / ASCAP Project. Produced by UJBH, Inc. Arrangements and Musical Production by Yaakov Hersher Vocals and final mix recorded at Armando's Studio. Video engineered and cut by Ed Vinson.

On Chayim's birthday, August 20, 2013, I wrote to him, "I'm so grateful for the grandsons you have given me. They are the extension of you loving me! Love, Momma"

Chayim's Children

My son's eldest son, Chanan, lived for 11 years with his maternal grandfather, who was a Holocaust survivor. I believe Zada had a tremendous impact on him. Chanan was the first grandbaby I took care of. He was born with spinal bifida and had 20 operations before age 20. Now he walks with a cane. He is now 27. He is my heart, the best part of my life. He has the wisdom of a wise old man, always thoughtful, kind, loving, and brilliant, a very special young man.

He was a brilliant scholar, an outstanding graduate and valedictorian of his Yeshiva high school in Miami. He had scholarships to Yeshivas throughout his college years. When he graduated, he went to a yeshiva in Minneapolis on a scholarship. They sent him to be a tutor at different yeshivas all over the East Coast for months at a time because he inspired the young Rabbis. He was so ahead of his class. Now he's living at a yeshiva in Flushing, New York. His Hebrew is like his English. He won't be a regular rabbi. He will become a Rosh Yeshiva in two years, like a principal of a school for student rabbis.

Chanan was fixed up for marriage up with a girl named Tova. I believe God arranged it. For their first date, he went to her house to meet her. Her father and one grandfather are rabbis. And she's brilliant, tiny, and beautiful. She wanted to be an accountant. She fell in love with Chanan. He's so considerate and kind. In New York, you have to take a test four times to become an accountant. Tova took the first test two weeks before their wedding. After the wedding, they went to Israel.

She became pregnant, but she went back to New York to take the next test even though she had morning sickness. She passed with a *96 percentile* out of almost 10,000 people. She works with PriceWaterhouse, and is working from home.

Tova got her first job at Price Waterhouse after the birth of their first child, Mindy, my fifth great-grandchild. She had her second child, Asher, just before Covid came. I'm proud to say I went to New York in 2020 for the baby's bris. Asher is named after his maternal grandfather, Zada, who was the survivor of Buchenwald, where he spent five years with his two brothers.

Chanan's wife Tova is the oldest of nine children, including twin sisters who are five, so Mindy plays with her aunts.

Chanan wrote this essay about his experiences when he was 13 or 14 years old. I think it shows remarkable ability and awareness, so I wanted to share it in my book:

> *"I believe in the power of ability. I believe people have the ability to achieve heights they have never dreamed of reaching. I am here on Earth on a journey, a quest with a goal. Though there might be obstacles, large and small…the adversity you challenge will just enhance your feeling of accomplishments once your goal has been met.*
>
> *"I was born with many complications all associated with a rare disease called Caudal Regression Syndrome. Many defects, abnormalities, and challenges come along with it. In a nutshell, Caudal Regression Syndrome is a rare disorder in which the lower portion of the spine is missing, therefore affecting much of the lower extremities. This disorder is very rare, affecting about one in every 350,000 babies. Fortunately, my case is very mild, and it turned out not to be life threatening, but only causes some physical abnormalities. Many times I will think to myself, why me? Why was I chosen out of 350,000 people to take on this challenge? I do not believe this was just mere coincidence. I believe there's got to be a reason for it because there is a reason for everything. I believe I also have the ability to achieve great heights just like any other person, despite my personal challenges.*
>
> *"A couple of years ago, I was experiencing a personal health issue*

which needed to be taken care of before I grew up. My parents and I were traveling across the United States visiting various doctors. The majority of the doctors we visited suggested that I undergo major surgery to my stomach which would change my life forever. After thinking this suggestion over with my family, I insisted that we tell the doctors "no" for now. Being that I was a very persistent and confident child, my parents agreed with me.

"Though the doctors all were sure that the issue was impossible to solve without surgery, I was still confident in my ability to solve the problem on my own. After a couple of months, I was able to achieve success. The doctors were all amazed at my abilities they never knew existed. Though it appears as if this was a true miracle, I believe I was only taking advantage of my perseverance, confidence, and true ability.

"Not only I, but each and every person has the capability to utilize the constructive powers of will and courage to beat personal challenges. Whether the challenge is as large as major surgery or as small as having a paper cut, I believe everybody has the power of ability. We all must be aware of this fantastic skill and make sure to take advantage of it, and we will be surprised at the amazing results."

My second grandson, Tuvia, is a very handsome young man. He looks just like my son Chayim. When he graduated from the yeshiva here, he went to Israel to study. Then there were attacks in Israel, and my son made him come back home at 18. His parents wouldn't let him return to Israel. He thought he was going back so he left everything there. He was so miserable here in Florida that his parents sent him to the school where Chanan was tutoring in Philadelphia. After three months, Tuvia turned himself around. He became so motivated. The following year, he got into a very good yeshiva in Lakewood. He did very well, he was very motivated, and he spent his third year in a yeshiva in Israel. He's back in the United States, now, and ready to continue studying in Lakewood, New Jersey, to become a rabbi. He's 24 now, and hopes to be matched for marriage this year.

When my third grandson, Moshe, was in junior high in his yeshiva, they selected him as the most considerate kid in the class. He's extremely bright, very outgoing, and very handsome, and still the most considerate kid. They had 100 kids in his junior high school, and they picked only 34 to go into the high school Yeshiva, the ones about whom they knew there would be no discipline problems, because they really cared about getting an education.

When Moshe was 12 years old, he wrote, "A leader is a person who teaches, leads and guides you on the right path in leading your life. He does not let the many difficult challenges in life get him down, and he always remains happy. My grandfather, Asher Greenberg, was a leader to his brothers during the Holocaust, his children and his friends. He was always happy and expressed a positive attitude. He was always happy and set a good example. He showed everyone how to accept Hashem's will with happiness and faith."

He's 6'3" now, 20 years old, and he looks just like my husband Alan. He's just like Chanan, an excellent student. He just got his bachelor's degree after two years in yeshiva. I asked him how he did it, and he said, "Nana, I study from 8 in the morning to 8 in the evening." He's planning to go study in Israel for a year. Moshe is a very motivated student and extremely smart and kind. I hope I live long enough to see what he becomes. He's hugely capable of doing so many things.

Now, with the coronavirus, Chanan is in New York, and Tuvia and Moshe are with my son Chayim and Michelle in Miami. Moshe is waiting to go to Israel, but because of the virus he plans to attend a very special old yeshiva in Brooklyn. Tuvia is going back to Lakewood to study in yeshiva.

When my son's three boys were growing up in Miami, I was so fortunate to live in the same city so I could see them each week. Unlike my daughters' children, who lived in other cities, so I would see them only once or twice a year, I would visit often with Chanan, Tuvia, and Moshe. I had the good fortune to be with them almost every weekend. As the children grew, the youngest one would get annoyed or say things to me like little children do. Chanan, who was seven years older, would always whisper to them and tell them a quiet word. I never understood what he was saying in Hebrew, but it was like magic. The boys would become so loving and respectful again.

After Chanan was an adult with children of his own, I asked him, "What did you say to your younger brothers? Tell me the word."

He replied, "Chesed."

Now I am studying Torah with Rabbi Smith at the Vi, and we often read the weekly lesson on the Torah portion written by the late Lord Rabbi Jonathan Sacks. In July 2020, his piece "The Covenant and Love," spoke about the meaning of Chesed, which is "extraordinary kindness." We show kindness to those to whom it is due. Rabbi Sacks wrote, "the very act of creation is an act of God's loving kindness." Chesed is an act of love, given out of the goodness of the giver. Chesed is unconditional grace.

My Brother Norman

My brother Norman was two years older than me, and I believe he was wounded emotionally when he was very young. My mother was unable to cope with a young aggressive male child. Her childhood was so dysfunctional that she repeated her mother's behavior. All these negative responses reinforced my brother's negativity.

Norman's life was totally negative in the way he saw himself. He hated school. The only thing that gave him positive reinforcement was his love for the sport of football. He grew very large and in junior high and high school, the kids named him "Truck." He was a tackle on the football team at Miami Beach High, and when he hit you, it felt like you were being hit by a truck. He became a hero as captain of the high school's successful team. The year he was captain, the school won the "All City" and "All State" championship over all the other high school football teams. That's what kept him in school.

College was not a place for him to continue. He was accepted at University of Florida, but quit to join the Army and play football, his passion. He was injured the first year and that finished his football years. He became very hostile, and it was difficult for him to find work.

I feel his negative self-image and anger developed very young. My mother's mother did the same thing to her youngest son, Uncle Boris. Mother's sister Helen also had a son, her youngest, who was dysfunctional. As Virginia Satir would say, they were wounded.

Norman married six months before I did to Sharon, the girl across the street. Both were extremely obese. Unfortunately, they never had children. They moved to California for several years, but were unsuccessful there as well.

Sharon became ill, and they returned to Miami. She was diagnosed with cancer, and they moved in with me until they bought a small house. After she died, Norman remained alone in their home.

Upon my suggestion, my husband Alan gave my brother a job at the Dutch Inn main office. He chauffeured and did whatever was needed. A legal secretary worked at the office, and she went after Norman. He remarried her six months later. She took advantage of him. She used up all his money and then divorced him a year later and got half his house. He had to get out!

He left Florida to go to Tennessee where his best friend was the coach at the University of Tennessee. Norman had been instrumental in his success as a high school football coach in Miami. After several years, the friend passed away, and Norman returned to Miami. Broken and lost, he rented a room in Miami and became a cab driver.

I recommended that he should go into therapy, which he did for five years, I believe, and I paid for it. He overcame his anger and was able to support himself for the rest of his life. He actually saved his money and purchased three cabbie licenses. He made money on training other cab drivers to drive the other two cabs.

I remember one night he came to my home and said, "I quit. I am retiring. I was just held up by a passenger with a gun to my head! It's a miracle I'm alive. I gave him my money! That's the end of driving a cab!"

Norman had diabetes and was still very overweight. He became ill, and I took him to my doctor who put him in a nursing home. While he was there, I visited him. I was fixing up his top drawer when I noticed a paper giving his three cab licenses to this lawyer that he knew. It said, "because he had no family." I questioned him and he said, "I had to sign it." I knew immediately that this was not legal. My mother and I were still alive and well.

I told Chayim, my son. He got a lawyer from downtown Miami. We gave the case to him. It took years of litigation and $10,000, but we won the case! Meanwhile, my mother died that year, so the three licenses belonged to me. They were worth a lot of money at that time.

Then Chayim's first son, Chanan, was born with spina bifada and needed many surgeries. I gave the money to my son. In fact, Chayim's father-in-law Asher's best friend had a string of cabs in Miami. Chaim arranged for his father-in-law to run the cabs, and my son received the revenue. This enabled him to pay for the medical operations his son Chanan needed for the next 10 to 15 years of his life, until he finished high school. This made the cost of Chanan getting the best medical treatment and operations—20 surgeries and counting—available to his parents. Meanwhile, Chayim and Michelle had two healthy sons to raise, and they could take care of everything thanks to my brother Norman's financial success.

My Life Story—Part 3

A Meditation

In 1980, I heard about a marriage encounter weekend, and I asked Alan to go with me. Several couples from Temple Beth Am were attending the retreat, which was held at a Howard Johnson hotel on 163rd Street in Miami. Several years after Alan and I divorced, I found his notebook with the things he had written that weekend. For decades since that time, I found it very difficult to look at what he had written, but recently, I reread it, and I feel for my children's sake that I need to put in my book some of what he wrote in a letter to me:

Dear Esther,

God gave me a gift when he gave me you. He must have said this man should receive love and tenderness. He is empty. He is void. I am truly sorry that I have not responded. Maybe God's gift to you is the children (their love of you, their love of God) and maybe God's gift to you is yet to come. Maybe I will learn. Maybe I will participate, and become involved in your beauty, in your tenderness, and accept it for its beauty, for its simplicity, for its richness. It is not designed to cause me harm (like my mother) but to enrich me, nourish me when I was sick, and, maybe, I hope and pray, I will respond, and I will not reject you.

I hope I will not be defensive. I will not be suspicious, but, as you say, 'open the doors' and let you in, and maybe respond with love, with kindness, with respect and admiration. Because, my beloved, you deserve it. You have paid a great price. Your love, your kindness, your concern for my well-being, so unselfish. The amazing things is that you have not changed. With all the walls I have put in our way, with all my rejection, you still keep pouring out love.

Do I see you and accept you as you really are? I'm sorry, my dear, I don't. This is my fault. I should. What you really are is God's gift to me. It's like a spring of water, like milk from a cow, all I have to do is drink from their live-giving nourishment. It is always there. I do not know how to avail myself of it.

Do you accept me as I really am? I am sure you do; how else could you live with me with all those rejections. You must have thought about leaving me many times, yet you didn't. Why? You understand my handicaps, you understand how crippled I am, and you have lived in hopes I would change with love.

In another part of the workbook, he wrote a second letter to me:

When I married you, how ill-equipped I was. When we first got married, I knew nothing about a constant relationship with a woman. I had known only fighting and hate, not love. I know that I married you because you were the most beautiful girl I had ever met and, more important, I sensed your deep, unselfish love for me. I wanted to respond but I did not know how. I never saw a man show love to his wife in the confines of a home. Only after much counseling—which you insisted I do—did my eyes open, and I did see your many talents and began to admire them and appreciate you and could begin to respond to your love.

I know you went through hell while I had to learn. The worst part was that I thought I knew everything, when, in fact, I knew nothing. I closed my eyes. I don't profess that I have learned so much, but now when I'm sober, I try to listen and understand. I do respect what you say. I therefore feel our marriage has gotten better. In our marriage's beginnings, my main motivation was money and being a success, not being a husband and father, but on business.

Our marriage only continued in a better way while his business was successful. When his business started to fail, little by little, so did our marriage. He treated me very badly, and fell into his old habits of drinking. Divorce and bitterness took over; other women and money issues took over.

However, I should explain that even when Alan went bankrupt and lost his hotel chain and his law practice, good parts of his life remained. He was still highly respected and known for all the good things he accomplished at Temple Beth Am and the Union of Hebrew Congregations of America. When we were a married couple, I asked Alan to put all his leadership and talent into our Temple, not being president of other organizations, like the Masons and bridge tournaments. In part of his note to me, he said, "I was content to continue the course you saw fit in order to have you and the children be a part of my leadership experiences, to share them with you and our family."

When Alan and I separated, I started to write. Until we divorced, and I moved to Grove Isle, a lovely condominium complex in Coconut Grove, I lived alone in our huge house in Kendall. I was by myself for the first time in my life.

I felt I needed to write down some of the wise, helpful ideas that I had learned in my studies, so that I could carry them with me and reach for and read them when I needed to. In my desperate attempt to adjust to the drastic changes in my life, I began writing a meditation. I learned that a meditation would be comforting to me when I was alone. I was searching for new alternatives for myself. I wasn't sure what my work would be like when I finished writing, but this is the essence of what I wrote:

> *This is my most important message of what I learned is that before I could have faith or see it in others, I had to have faith in myself. I had to have trust in myself before I could trust others. I had to accept myself first before I could accept other people completely.*

Esther with Hugh and Susie Beeler, Chayim and Michelle Kessler, and Pam and Ira Brenner

Esther's first picture of her five oldest grandchildren before Tuvia and Moshe were born: Eric, Tamara, Chanan, Nina, and Ali

Esther with Tuvia, Tamara, Pam and Chanan

Esther with Ali, Tamara, Hugh, Nina, Susie, and Eric in Savannah

Chayim's little boys—
Moshe, Tuvia, and
Chanan—in Boca

And little Eric Beeler

Chayim and Michelle with Tuvia, Moshe, and Chanan at Disney World

Chayim with Tuvia and Chanan

Esther with Nina and Tamara at Nina's Bat Mitzvah

Tamara and Nina

OPPOSITE: The family at Ali's Bat Mitzvah: Chayim, Hugh, Susie, Eric, Michelle, Nina, Tamara, Ali, Ira, Pam, Esther, Moshe, Chana, and Tuvia

Susie, Ali and Esther at Ali's Bat Mitzvah

Esther with Nina and Tamara at Ali's Bat Mitzvah

Ali holds the microphone for Uncle Chayim at her Bat Mitzvah

Esther on an Alaska cruise with Ali and Eric, celebrating Ali's college graduation and Eric's high school graduation

OPPOSITE: The whole family gathered at Eric's Bar Mitzvah: Hugh, Esther, Susie, Ali, Ira, Chanan, Nina, Tamara, Michelle, and Chayim. Front row: Aiden, Moshe, Tuvia, Pam, and Eric

Ali, Nina and Tamara at Eric's Bar Mitzvah

Eric at his high school graduation with Susie, Hugh, Esther, and Ali

RIGHT: Eric was a page in Washington, DC, and met President Obama

Chayim's sons—Tuvia, Chanan, and Moshe—at Chanan's Bar Mitzvah

BELOW: As adults

Esther with Tuvia at his high school graduation

ABOVE: Chanan and Tova's engagement party: Moshe, Michelle, Chayim, Esther, Chanan, Tova, and her parents, Rabbi and Mrs. Fink

Tova and Chanan's wedding

Tova on her wedding day

BELOW: Tova, Chanan, and baby Asher at his bris

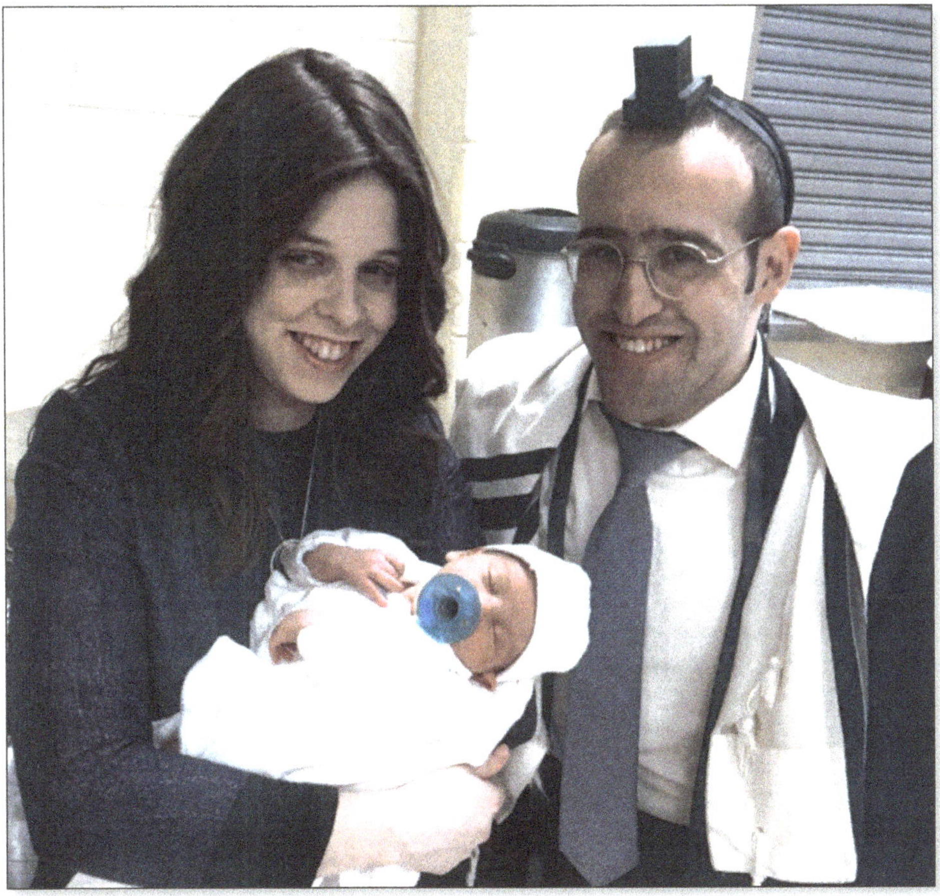

Esther and Moshe at Asher's bris

ABOVE: Chayim sings inspirational Jewish music

BELOW: Chayim and Esther

THE GREAT-GRANDCHILDREN

Nina's son Aiden

Nina's son Amiel

Tamara's daughter Rifka

Tamara's son Abraham

Chanan's daughter Mindy, age 2

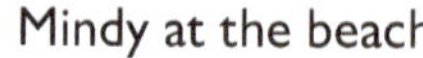

Mindy at the beach

Chanan's
son Asher

Esther, Marge Davis, and Dallas Weinstein played tennis
and had lunch together every week for 20 years

BELOW: Esther's high school girlfriends and their mothers had
a 40 years reunion: Irene Farkas, Ida Schulman, Esther, Delores
Farkas Bramson, and Rita Stein and her mother

Esther at home at Grove Isle

Esther at Esalen

OPPOSITE: Esther's Temple Beth Am chavurah friends

Esther and Herman Pitter

OPPOSITE, TOP: Esther and her second husband, Bill Saltzman

OPPOSITE, LEFT: Bill as a young man

OPPOSITE, RIGHT: Bill when he and Esther first met

Bill and Esther's wedding

Bill and Esther's wedding with Ali, Hugh, Susie, and Eric welcoming Grandpa Bill to the family. Each guest received a small framed message that read: *Two lives are made into one, Two halves are made whole, Two friends are made husband and wife, Esther and Bill, June 13, 1999.*

Bill at Grove Isle

OPPOSITE: Bill and Esther's wedding:
Cousin Dr. Edward Kaplan, Bill, Esther,
cousin Philip Kaplan, Shirley Kaplan,
and Sue Kaplan and her children

Esther in Toronto

BELOW: Esther and Bill's home in Boca Raton

Celebrating Pam's 50th birthday in Boca

Esther and Hy Kopel on a cruise with his family from Brisbane, Australia: Honor, Robert, Hy, Esther, Marge, and Jonathan

With the family for Seder in Boca. Front row: Chanan, Pam, Aiden, and Nina. Back row: Tamara, Esther, Hy

On safari in South Africa

Hy and Esther at the Cape of Good Hope

After the Divorce & After the Accident

I sold my home in Kendal in 1986, and moved to Building 3 at Grove Isle in Coconut Grove. My companion there was an educated, handsome man named Herman Pitter, a retired accountant almost 10 years my senior. He was my significant other, my first relationship after my divorce. Herman lived with me at Grove Isle, but he had a depression mentality about money so I never wanted to marry him. We had a terrible car accident in 1989 when someone being chased by the police hit our car.

Healing from the accident took a very long time. I went through the windshield and had to have plastic surgery. I lost many of my teeth and broke my hip. I didn't walk again for about two years. It was all very difficult. Herman and I stayed together for a couple of years while I healed, but then I knew it was time for us to break up, and I ended the relationship.

As I emerged from my depression after the accident, I wrote this poem for myself:

The light is always shining within me.
Even in the face of the darkness, the sun will shine for me.

I must think positive and I will see positive things happen.
Only by thinking positive will I see the positive sides of everything.
(No one can do it for me.)

Drawing a rainbow reminds me that If I look for it and
Remember it is somewhere to be found—I will find it.
The Sun is all around me, and it is up to me to see
The rainbow in my life.

I was single for seven years, including my time working at the Four Freedoms as a social worker before I met my second husband.

My Second Husband, William "Bill" Saltzman from Toronto, Canada

I was living in Grove Isle and working at the Four Freedoms on Miami Beach. An old friend of 30 years, Joyce Roman (Lerner) was living at the Arlen House on Miami Beach. She invited me to spend New Year's 1998 with her at her apartment. The building was having a New Year's Eve party, and there were several single men she wanted me to meet.

Bill Saltzman and his brother-in-law Harry had rented an apartment for six months to spend the winter in Florida. They came to Miami from Toronto in Harry's Cadillac. Joyce introduced me to Bill and insisted that he sit next to me. It was an instant love affair. For two hours, we never left our seats except to dance. I gave him my friend's phone number to reach me. The next day and the next day, he never called. When he did, he explained that his brother-in-law Harry and he were walking to pick up a newspaper the next morning, and Harry tripped and broke both his elbows, and had to be operated on immediately.

Bill finally called my friend to contact me, and the rest was history. We had six months together. Harry was flown back to Canada, and Bill remained in Miami Beach.

After we dated four months, my son told me that I should marry Bill, not live with him, because I had seven grandchildren—so how could he explain my living with Bill. That is what Bill wanted, too, but I kept saying "no."

But I went to Toronto after Bill returned home, and my son and his wife Michelle planned a wedding for us at Grove Isle, where I lived 13 years. They gave us a beautiful wedding in June, 1999, and for almost two years, Bill and I continued to live at Grove Isle in my apartment.

Bill had a beautiful condo in Toronto, and we spent six months in Toronto, six months in Miami, and six months in Toronto, because Bill had to maintain his Canadian citizenship to keep up his health insurance.

We were looking for a house. We both had always lived in houses. We saw nothing in Miami, but we both loved a small house in a complex in Boca Raton, Florida. Bill loved the small pool. Coming from Canada, he was so excited about the pool. He enjoyed it all year long. He loved the winters in Florida, and I volunteered for 12 years at the Boca Community Hospital. I also became a life member and president of the Hadassah Chapter in Boca.

Each summer we went to Toronto, Canada, to his apartment. Every six months, I became a snowbird, living in Canada, and sometimes visiting there during the winter for family events. Bill was a Conservative Jew, and his father had started a Conservative shul in Toronto. Bill was a past president, as was his son. Bill had two children, a twin sister, and a million friends in Toronto. It was a wonderful life as long as it lasted. We were together from 1989 to 1996, but his son robbed us of our last year of marriage.

I did not know my marriage was doomed from the beginning. I didn't realize Bill's children resented me and him living in Boca and spending his money. Bill's son did not like this arrangement. He felt Bill was spending his (the son's) future money on me, limiting what would remain for him, what would be left for his own retirement. That's when my life changed. Bill's son and his wife were trying to figure out how to get rid of me and keep Bill in Canada without me. Bill's twin sister lived in Canada, and she was in her 80s.

In the summer of 2005, Bill developed severe back pain. His Canadian medical coverage was good only if he lived six months of the year in Canada, so when he needed surgery to relieve his chronic back pain, we returned to Canada.

It is very painful to write about what happened next. On the operating table during the surgery, Bill had a heart attack. Thank God, he was revived, and we spent several months in a convalescent home together.

Bill was not able to get health insurance to return to Florida for six months. The son and his wife decided they had to get rid of me. At the time, we were both staying in his son's home. The son had lost his wife's retirement money. I was aware of that. They decided that since his wife was 65, she could retire and care for my husband and get paid for it. That was their plan, but I was in the way. His son would not allow Bill to return to Florida.

Thank God, when I married Bill I got a pre-nuptial agreement, but Bill's son told me I had to leave his house and leave Toronto. He said he and his wife would take care of Bill in their home. It was the worst day of my life! This son and his wife had planned how to get rid of Bill's American wife, so his wife could collect weekly pay from his estate to care for him. My husband Bill couldn't do anything; he could not fight his son. He had to remain in Canada for now, and his son had power of attorney over his name. Bill arranged for a ticket, and I returned to our home in Boca alone. I never saw my husband again!

The saddest days of my life began. I was not allowed to see my husband again after I returned to Boca. This horrible son and his wife refused to let me talk to him or see him. No phone calls were allowed. It's upsetting even to speak about the next year.

I remember my grandson Chanan was 14 years old and studying Torah. He asked me what happened to Grandpa Bill. I told him and in his wisdom, he told me what he learned: A father can do this to a son, but a son cannot do this to a father.

Almost a year later, in 1999, I received a phone call from Canada from Bill's grandson Mark informing me that Bill, my husband, had passed away in his sleep that night. His son had destroyed his father and taken his wife and his life away!

I had an amazing experience I want to share with you. In 2019, I bought myself a walker and I kept it in the car. It had a pocket to put things in. I keep it folded in my car; I don't need it. I use it if I go to the mall, because I can't walk so far. One day I went to the mall and took out my walker, and something fell out of the pocket—I never keep anything in it because you have to fold it up.

It was my Bill's yarmulke. He'd been dead 20 years. It had a monogram, William Saltzman. I bought that car after he died. I had been using that walker for a year; nothing was in it. He put it there. I know he did. He wanted me to know he was thinking about me. Some people may not believe the story I have just told, but believe me it happened.

We had a wonderful second marriage for a very short time.

Single in Boca

About three years after I returned to Florida, to my home in Boca, I met Hy Kopel. He was a jeweler born in Johannesburg, South Africa. He had come to the United States about 30 year earlier, when he met a woman in Israel who invited him to New York for a visit. He married her and lived in New York until they moved to Boca. She passed away before I met him.

He was working in a jewelry store where I had some jewelry repaired, and he talked to me. I went in to fix my watch, and there was a sign in the shop with a silver frame saying that the store also would do engraving. I had a bracelet that I was wearing, and I thought about having the back of the name plate engraved that I am allergic to penicillin, and I have two stents in my heart. He said to me, "Shana madela, with so much tsuris" (beautiful girl with so much trouble). That's when I realized he was Jewish, like myself. We started to talk, and he took my telephone number so he could call and tell me when to pick up the bracelet.

When he called me, he asked if he could take me out to dinner. I agreed, and that was our first date. After our dinner date, when we were on the phone, I learned more about him. I suggested he get out of the HMO he had joined. The HMO told him he was a borderline diabetic and gave him something he could use to check his blood. He told me he had problems with his right eye, and the HMO told him to get glasses.

He also told me he had a cyst in his kidney, and that he had colon cancer and prostate cancer several years before he joined the HMO, and they were not treating him. So, I got him out of the HMO and into Medicare, enabling him to get different specialist doctors for each of his medical problems. In fact, I got him to see a specialist eye doctor and found out he had macular degeneration. They have been treating him with shots in his eye for 10 years, and that has kept him from going blind.

For over 13 years, after my second husband died, Hy was my significant other. He lived at Century Village in Boca, and I had my own three-bedroom home. Several years after we met, Hy invited me on a trip to South Africa for three weeks. He came from Johannesburg. We stayed at his brother's apartment there, and I met his whole family, including his sister's and brother's children. We took a trip to Cape Town, one of the most beautiful scenic places I've ever been to in my life. It's a breathtaking city with mountains on the ocean.

Once, when Hy was in the hospital in Florida, I wrote the following letters to my children. His serious illness made it important for me to think about those I love, their values, and my values.

Dear Chayim,

I'm sitting in the hospital with Hy. I feel he will get better as soon as they know how to treat him. I was reading an article here in the hospital, and it made me think about myself and my family. I was taught by example to love, to heal and truly give back. I guess that's why I became a social worker. My mother's family taught me that. It was their Jewish values. That's what Judaism teaches.

You are an example to your sons and clients. You teach the values of Orthodox Judaism to your clients, changing their lives for the better. You have taught your children well about kindness, and I have prioritized education and the pursuit of knowledge. Chanan is a perfect example. Tuvia and Moshe will follow the same path they have been taught. I was thinking about what my legacy would be.

My most important legacy, I think, will be the grandchildren and what they have accomplished in their lives.

I wanted to share this with you,

All my love,

Momma

Dear Pam,

I'm sitting in the hospital with Hy. They don't know what went wrong that his pressure goes so low. I feel he will be better in a few days, please God!

I was reading an article here in the hospital, and it made me think about myself and my family. I was taught by example especially by Aunt Sophie to love, to heal and truly give back. That came from the Jewish values the family had been taught. I taught my children kindness, and I prioritized education and the pursuit of knowledge. You certainly achieved those values. As a mother and teacher and as a person of worth! You are respected and loved wherever you live, especially by the several hundred children you've taught music to over the years.

I understand myself more of why I had to help Nina achieve my values. She was your daughter, and she allowed me to. I saw the second chance she needed, whatever it took, and gave it to her. The most important thing is that Nina accomplished it all.

I was thinking about what my legacy will be. My most important legacy, I think, will be the grandchildren and what they accomplish in their lives. I wanted to share this with you,

Love,

Momma

Dear Susie and Hugh,
I'm sitting in the hospital with Hy. They don't know what went wrong that his pressure goes so low. I feel he will be better in a few days, please God!

I was reading an article here in the hospital, and it made me think about myself and my family. I was taught by example especially by Aunt Sophie to love, to heal and truly give back, from my mother's family on. You and Hugh are the kind of parents who taught your children well because you were both taught those values, especially kindness. Ali and Eric are perfect examples of what they were taught. You work teaching children changed their lives for the better. You helped them believe that they can achieve anything because you believed in each child's capabilities.

I was thinking about what my legacy will be. My most important legacy, I think, will be the grandchildren and what they accomplish in their lives. I wanted to share this with you,
Love,
Momma

Hy and I were together from 2000 to 2013, when we broke up. In April 2014, when I was no longer with him, I surprisingly found that becoming single again had led to some improvements in my life. I no longer had to get home or be committed to anyone. I made appointments with new and old friends. I did the things that I felt like doing when I felt like doing them, depending on where I was at the time.

My life was full of surprises, and I was happier. For example, I could park my car and walk to the beach for an hour as the sun went down. However, the weekends were hard for me. I had always spent them with Hy. Now, I had to plan for Saturdays and Sundays on my own.

For several years, I volunteered for hospice, where I learned how to console others by listening to them and by reflecting on the legacy of those they mourned. Then, I read in the newspaper that they were seeking volunteers for four hours on Saturdays at the Children's

Museum in Boca. I loved it! I was in contact with very small children and their parents, and the kids were so cute. I sold gifts in the gift shop to raise money for the museum. I told my son that driving to Miami to see the family on Sunday—once a week—was all I needed. I had found my independence again.

Living in Boca for 16 years, I was next door to the Morikami Japanese Gardens. I was grateful to have such extraordinary beauty and peaceful serenity at my back door.

Today I am living back in Miami. In 2016, I moved into independent living at the Vi, a beautiful high-rise in Aventura, where I have been a member of the resident council and chair of the Food and Beverage Committee for the past three years. I am very happy at almost 90 to still have some responsibility for making other people's lives better.

I moved to the Vi in 2016 from Boca with my 40 bromeliads, which grow now on my porch here. When I had them in Boca, I always saw a chameleon in my garden. And when I unpacked my plants here, something moved. It was the chameleon. He came with me to the Vi.

Recently, I found a short poem I wrote for a class in 1983:

> "Oh, Lord, there is so much to live for, Heaven can wait.
> I'd rather stay here."

My Life Story—Part 4

MY WORKING LIFE AND THE PEOPLE I HELPED

First job: Jewish Vocational Services

My first job after my divorce was with Jewish Vocational Services. I was a social worker for all of South Dade. I would arrange to have nurse's aides work in senior citizens' homes. I hired aides with green cards and matched them with senior citizens who called needed services. I brought community services to people and helped them in their homes.

Then I went to work for a private company so I could continue to get health insurance. I was hired by Medicare Home Health as a social worker doing home assessments when people need to be referred to services. I loved the job, but the government closed the agency for some infractions they committed that weren't related to my work.

Many of the people I'd worked with for that job were elderly and spoke only Spanish. My Spanish was not very good, and I wanted to communicate. When I lived at Grove Isle, which is a beautiful condominium complex in Coconut Grove, the staff included young Hispanic men who parked the cars. I hired one of the young men for $5 an hour to help with my Spanish patients for a half-day each week. He learned English, and he loved helping people and doing translations for me.

Then I had to look for another job, and my credentials were perfect to join a private health company that received a government grant to train aides to relieve people who were caregivers for Alzheimer's patients. I used to hire aides and put them in jobs for Jewish Vocational Services. The University of Miami would train them to work with Alzheimer's patients so they could give a reprieve to the caregivers. This government grant established the program, and it's now in every city in the United States, paid for by the government to allow caregivers to place their loved ones who are Alzheimer's patients in care for several hours, taking some of the burden away and keeping the caregivers from needing to be hospitalized.

Then I had my car accident in 1989, and I couldn't work for two years.

People I Helped as a Social Worker at Four Freedoms

When I went back to work, I became the social worker at the Four Freedoms, a 15-story high, low-cost housing building on Collins Avenue and 33rd Street in Miami Beach. The building had 150 apartments for senior citizens. I worked there for Jewish Vocational Services (JVS), and I had an office in the lobby. I was there to assist the senior citizens who lived in the building with community services and personal needs. All the tenants were receiving government assistance.

My job was to help residents obtain social services if they were eligible. If they could no longer care for themselves, I had to make arrangements to move them to nursing homes. I would make appointments with the tenants to help them with their health needs or their financial needs. I worked there for seven years. I loved my job, and I have hundreds of stories of my experiences with the elderly residents and their lives and deaths.

Part of my job was arranging for activities for the residents. I realized that tenants had to take care of their own meals, and the biggest problem I had was that many of them were not eating properly. Some of them did not have the money to buy necessary nutritious food.

I contacted Jewish Vocational Services where I had worked before and put together a meal program in my building. I knew from my previous job with JVS that one of its programs had special sites where people could come and get a hot, nutritious meal, so I arranged for the Four Freedoms to be on the food program. Then the people there received a hot meal every evening. The food was cooked daily and brought in, and we provided a hot lunch for one dollar. The meal program served its purpose in health and socialization. People got out of their apartments and met the neighbors. On Friday, the religious tenants had a Sabbath candle lighting and short service. It was beautiful to observe. I was so proud to be part of the things I accomplished there, and I felt I was truly changing people's lives for the better.

I also arranged for Meals on Wheels at the Four Freedoms House for lunch for one dollar. It was very rewarding for me to see 60 to 100 people enjoying a hot lunch each day at the building where they lived. This meal program gave them a place to get out of their apartment at noon, and have a hot, nutritious meal. The person who delivered the food gave them someone to talk to each day.

I noticed early on that the elderly Jewish tenants were very proud and didn't like to ask for help. The more recent tenants were Russian elderly and Cuban-born, and they seemed to expect or even demand anything that was available to them. I tried to make sure that everyone got all the help they needed. The apartments were one-room efficiencies, and each tenant lived alone.

I would like to share several of my experiences with my elderly tenants. When my grandchildren were young, they loved hearing some of these stories. It made them laugh.

Many of the people in the Four Freedoms had no money, so I helped them get on Medicaid according to their income. Most were very proud. Most belonged to HMOs for health care. But I noticed that the tenants who belonged to the Humana HMO died, and the tenants who had their choice of doctors under Medicaid and had private doctors were still alive. The people in the HMOs had Spanish doctors whom the residents couldn't understand. The Spanish people had English doctors. So there were no conversations either way. Our residents kept seeing doctors they couldn't communicate with. The people with HMOs kept dying because the HMOs weren't doing the right testing to determine how to extend people's lives.

I would suggest to residents to quit the HMO, and I would get them into Medicare by filling out papers for them. That way they could go to doctors the HMO didn't permit. I began to keep a long list of people who belonged to HMOs. IF they were eligible to go on Medicaid, I tried to assist them. I noticed that the Jewish patients were not looking for charity and would shy away from any handouts. The Russian and Cuban seniors were extremely interested in everything that they could benefit from that was free! I helped all the eligible tenants get out of HMOs and become Medicaid patients. Then they could pick doctors of their choice—any specialists who accepted Medicaid—thereby prolonging their lives.

I knew a young brilliant heart doctor, a very fine cardiologist, Dr. Solomon, on 41st Street in Miami Beach. He was very ambitious and was starting his own practice. I would refer my clients to him when they went on Medicaid. Several times, we worked with children to help obtain the medications they needed. I remember Irene, a dressmaker. I hadn't seen her for several weeks, and one day she told me she had gone to Dr. Solomon, and he put her in the hospital for open heart surgery.

When I changed people to Medicaid so they could go to a specialist, I'd send them to him. This saved many people's lives. One lady had a heart attack and went to Dr. Solomon. He did open heart surgery. Her son from New York came to thank me and said that I gave her life. If she had stayed in the HMO, she would have died. I felt I saved many residents' lives when I was at the Four Freedoms.

I well remember some of the individuals I helped.

I helped a lady named Sonia who lived in Freedom Tower. She had been a dressmaker, and she went dancing with her boyfriend every weekend. She belonged to an HMO, and told me the doctor was Spanish and she couldn't understand him. I suggested that she allow me to do the paperwork for her to become a Medicaid patient since she met the requirements. She needed to request paperwork to get out of the Humana HMO. The only problem was that the HMO paid for her medication for a small fee.

Sonia said she had one son who made a good living and was helping her with anything she needed financially. I recommend that she see my doctor, a cardiologist, whose office was close to her apartment. He accepted Medicaid patients. The following year or so, Sonia had pains in her chest. She was put in Mt. Sinai Hospital immediately and had open heart surgery. Several weeks later, Sonia's son came to my office and thanked me for saving his mother's life. Sonia showed me the dress she was making for her granddaughter's wedding.

And there was a resident named Sophie who was 90. She had macular degeneration and was losing her sight when I met her. As the years progressed, she was almost hit by a car when crossing the street. I was afraid when she went out that she wouldn't be able to get back. She told me that at night she slept on sweaters and things piled up beside the bathroom so she would be able to find the toilet. She was no longer able to care for herself. I knew I would have had to place her in a nursing home. I knew it would kill her to move. She had been in Freedom Towers for 10 years.

I went into the main office at Freedom Tower to see if she had a relative. I found a grandson, a doctor living in Tampa. I phoned him on my own money (this was in the time before cellphones made long distance calls free). I told him I was a social worker in his grandmother's building, and that I was concerned because her sight was failing so fast that I would have to put her in a nursing home.

I said to him, this is why I'm calling you, to suggest that perhaps you could find a place near you—then maybe you could visit her, and everything would be better. I waited and waited for a reply. He said, "No I cannot do that." I was taken by surprise by his negative answer.

I asked, "Why wouldn't that be possible?" I was also surprised by his explanation. He said, "It's a very personal thing. My mother and I don't speak to each other. If I bring my grandmother, here my mother will know where I am." He told me she was not aware of where he was living.

I thought about that and answered, "Could I suggest, since there are so many little cities around Tampa, if you could find a place nearby outside of Tampa that would take her, would you consider it? Then you could visit her with your children as often as you can. He took my phone number and said he would consider it. Three months later, he called me and said, "I found a place in a little town an hour from Tampa. I'm making arrangements, and they have a bed for her. Tell her I'm coming to take her."

Several weeks later, there was a knock on my office door. In the doorway was Sophie and her grandson, arm in arm, coming to say goodbye to me. The funny thing was that the grandson looked so much like Sophie. He also had red hair like her, and he's five feet, six inches tall, short like her. She said, "This is my grandson. He's taking me. And everything in my apartment, I'm leaving to you." It was all rags, but it is a lovely story.

When my three grandsons were little, they loved my stories. Well, little kids love do-do stories, so I told them about a man at Freedom Tower. One day the manager came into my office and said that the elevator had "B.M" in it. I needed to go to every floor—we had 15 stories—and see where it was coming from. I had success on the fifth floor. A man in his 80s.

This man was single, and he used to be in the Navy. He was losing his sight and had no family nearby. The apartment was a mess, and he was always in trouble because it was so dirty, but he couldn't see or control his bowels. He wouldn't let a maid in his apartment because he had been on a ship and took care of himself nicely before this. He had lived in the building for 15 years, totally alone. He was unable to stay in the building because he could not care for himself, but he was eligible to go to a nursing home on Medicaid. I arranged for him to go to a nursing home with meals.

Then, the manager told me that a woman in the building was hoarding books. She belonged to a book club, and the books just kept coming. I told her we had to take the books out because they were creating a fire hazard. She had books piled all the way to the ceiling, with just a passageway to get into the apartment. All around the bed were books to the ceiling. There was no room for her to lay down on the bed. I had two maintenance men who worked in the building take all the books out. My job was to get them out and solve the fire hazard so she could remain a resident.

Sarah was an 89-year-old from Israel. She had no family in the United States. She came to Canada at 18 to join her sister. They moved to New York where she married a Holocaust survivor. That's about all I knew about her. She was a Kosher Jewish woman. On my day off, I would bring my grandson Chanan to the Four Seasons building, which was across the street from the Boardwalk along the beach. I would take Chanan for a walk. He was two years old, and I'd bring a toy that he pushed. Before we left, we would walk across the street to get some Kosher candy and use the bathroom at Sarah's apartment. We became very close friends. In fact, when I got tickets for a show, I would take Sarah. On my birthday, Sarah walked over the 41st Street Bridge to the bakery in the June heat in Florida to bring a cake to my office! How I appreciated her love.

But Sarah was getting very frail and ill, and I knew very soon I would have to move her to a nursing home. One day, I went into the building office to get information on her closest relative, a niece in Israel. Sarah's parents were buried in Israel and so were her siblings. Sarah would quietly tell me that her dream was to be buried in Israel close to her family. So I called her niece in Israel, and she told me more about Sarah.

Sarah had one son from a very painful marriage. Her son was on drugs. He robbed Sarah and took her valuable possessions. No wonder she never talked about him.

The niece explained that she had two nephews, her sister's sons. She brought them to America when they were small. Several years ago, Sarah had lost touch with them. The nephews were in New York trying to locate her. Her niece gave me their phone numbers. When I called her New York family, the nephew I spoke to was a religious school teacher who blessed me for calling him. He said Sarah had given so much to his family. He said he would call her and arrange to come see her as soon as possible.

He did just that. And he brought her to New York and to his daughter's wedding, and later arranged with my help to place her in the Kosher Jewish nursing home where my brother was living. Fortunately, I was able to see Sarah and my brother each week for several years.

The nephew took care of her finances. One day the nephew's wife called me to tell me Sarah had died, and her nephew was on a plane to Israel with Sarah's body. He arranged for her funeral and bought a plot in Israel so she could be buried with her siblings and her parents. That was always Sarah's dream! For seven years, I became like her daughter.

To me, being able to help people and make a difference in their lives gave tremendous purpose and meaning to the work I did throughout my career, and it was important in my personal life, as well.

I learned to apply what I had learned about humanistic psychology and value clarification strategies. I was trained to make every attempt to lift the spirits and morale of the seniors I worked with whenever possible. When we deal with human beings, we must expect problems, and we have to see people as human beings and not expect perfection. I am constantly aware of the love within them, even when there is conflict or difficulty. As a social worker, I always hoped that we could resolve any conflicts—when you deal with people, that is part of the nature of the job—and I focused on the positive.

Helping My Friends

I was always very glad when I could help my friends and neighbors.

Lillie Kimler, a neighbor when I was a child, was my mother's best friend. She became part of my extended family. Lillie got a divorce and went to New York to stay with her aging mother. She had a son, about 12, and a daughter, Marlene, 17, who was a senior in high school. Lillie was depressed, and received electric shock treatment in New York and had to remain there. Her daughter wanted to return to high school in Miami. I brought her back to live with me so she could go to school and wait for her mother to return home. Marlene attended the University of Miami and became a dental assistant. She eventually married a young man who worked for my husband for 10 years until they, too, divorced.

When I was married and had gone back to school to get my social work degree, I was also able to help my cleaning lady, Rose, who was raising three daughters alone. Her oldest child was about 13 years old. I suggested to Rose that she might want to take her daughter to a gynecologist and discuss the facts of life and birth control with her. At the time I was working at Jackson Memorial Hospital for my social work degree, and I saw so many black teenagers having babies. As a social worker, I had worked with many Black families where the mother was raising their children's children. I was so happy I could help Rose raise her daughters.

About 20 years later, Rose called me. She thanked me for how I helped her. Her daughters had finished high school, and her eldest daughter was finishing college with a degree as a teacher.

I became close friends with one of my neighbors. We both had three children of similar ages. She had a husband who was similar to mine, not very sensitive. We became very close, since our lives were similar at the time. We didn't realize how much we shared, but we thrived on each other's kindness. After perhaps 15 years of close friendship, she told me that her father, who owned the business that her husband worked for, had fired her husband! The father had to protect his business. I knew her problems, but she said her husband was going to move their family up north where he came from.

I spoke with Alan, who had gone into the hotel business by then after practicing law and who had a thriving new hotel chain. My question was that if my friend moved away from her parents, what would happen to her family.

I suggested to my husband that perhaps he could give her husband a business contract for our hotels throughout the United States, so they could remain in their home as usual, and he could get a job. Her husband then could join another company since he would come to work for them with the contract for our hotels in hand. This worked for maybe eight to ten years while our hotels thrived. But then, business became very bad, and our hotels were in danger of going bankrupt. My friend's husband sped up the demise of our business by cancelling his contract with the hotels. This ungrateful man started the collapse of our hotels with his actions.

I never told my friend what her husband did. You take a risk, I learned, when you help another person. I also realize that most people are more considerate and thoughtful than her heartless husband. She is a wonderful person, loving and kind.

In time, Alan and I had some hard times and, as I wrote about earlier, we were divorced in 1986. I have forgiven him for our hard times. I think leaving law and going into business led to a lot of pressure. I realize he stopped reaching for his higher self and his connection with God, and then he turned to drinking instead.

When I was studying family therapy, I was assigned to write a letter to someone about how I had created, enabled, or allowed that person to do things that unknowingly set him or her up for me to reject them. Now, I was trained and expected to have more knowledge and insight.

For the class, I wrote (but never delivered) this letter to Alan:

Dear Alan,

For 27 years, I tried to change you into becoming a lover, not a fighter. I spent all my energy and time trying to change you to stop drinking. I really have patience and tenacity. I really believed I could change you.

After many years in therapy for myself, I realized that you would not change, that you wouldn't admit that you were an alcoholic. You were so deceitful that you blamed me for your drinking and denied the problem. I wanted you to be perfect like the family I presented to the outside world. I made such a pretty picture.

You gave me all the material things I could possibly want, but you were unable to love me. I had to love you, but you do not know how to love. In a relationship, you have to be able to love and to be able to be loved. That part of our relationship—you loving me—you stopped several years ago. You tried again when you stopped fighting with me—but people don't change. You went back to your (drinking)… when problems started. When I finally stopped loving you, there was no relationship. That was the sum and substance of the end of our marriage.

I feel the future will be richer for me when I find someone to love me and someone I will love again. I deserve that kind of love. I am not afraid to love again because that's the beauty in the world that is ahead of me.

In my workshops and classes, I learned that you can find your higher self by forgiving yourself first, letting go of anger, and trusting in God again, becoming open to God again, Alan learned this behavior, drinking to escape, from his mother. She had been a drinker. I was so fortunate to get my Orthodox values from my family. From their suffering in Europe, they kept their values.

Through the years, I saved the loving letters I received from my children. Here are letters (birthday greetings and a Valentine's Day card) they wrote in 1971 when they were teenagers, and we were living in our big house in Kendal. When each of my children reached the age to express their love for me, I saved their letters and framed them. I didn't understand in those years why it meant so much to me. I realize now that I was starved for love. My husband was not capable of giving love, only receiving love, but I knew that all three of our children were capable of loving. I saw it in their actions and in the letters they wrote to me as they were growing up.

Pam wrote me a birthday poem:

Although we're several hundred miles apart,
A feeling grows strong in my heart.
(I don't know what I'd do without you.)
Your thoughtful, loving family desires
Your everlasting giving that never tires.
Hope this day brings happiness and peace
I love you with all my heart and that shall never cease!

Susie wrote this on Valentine's Day that year:

Mom, I want to wish you a very Happy Valentine's Day. This card expresses the feelings I have toward you. I know that you always want the best for me, and I usually rebel against you. But, I really appreciate everything you do for me. Not too many mothers care about their daughters the way you care for me. I'm just beginning to realize what you do for me. It's hard to express this verbally, so I thought I would write it to you. Take care of yourself and speak to you soon,

Love Always, Susie

And this was my birthday card from Robbie, also in 1971:

Happy Birthday to a mother who always shares a piece of her heart.

Full of kindness, love, and charity since the very start.

Sometimes I lose my temper and act very immature,

But deep inside I know I love you, and these foolish ways will cure.

I'm sorry I'm not there to share my love on this important day,

But I feel that expressing myself in this letter is just as important a way.

I hope this day will be filled with peace, no fighting should be heard.

There's only one way to express the kind of mother you are:

Fantastic is the word!!

After our divorce, I was living alone in our large, six-bedroom home in Kendall. My daughter Susie suggested that I invite a friend of hers, David, to live with me. He had gone to college with her and had graduated and gotten a job in Miami. He stayed with me for four years. He was wonderful company and no trouble. He even took care of the pool at the house.

Some 34 years later, David got back in touch with Susie through Facebook. He had recently moved to the West Coast of Florida and bought a condo. Susie suggested that he could go see her daughter, my granddaughter, Ali, play in a tennis tournament in Ft. Myers, near his home. He said he would love to go. He kept telling Susie how much he loved me. He asked how I was and told her all the things I did to make him feel good while he lived with me.

Susie told him that by then I was 82 and lived in Boca Raton, and I wanted to go see Ali play tennis. It was her senior year, and she was captain of her tennis team, but I had no one to drive with to get there.

David told her he could drive to Boca Raton, get me the day before, take me to the tennis match, and then drive me home. I slept over in his condo after the match, and the next day he drove us to Boca and spent two days at my house. I had the pleasure of his company and took him all over Boca. I remembered that he had known my mother, my brother, and my aunts, who had all passed away. I remembered that he used to paint very well. I gave him my easel for painting, since I had never used it, and he took it home in his car. He said it changed his life. He started painting everything he loved in nature, sending the paintings as gifts, and selling them.

When I lived in Boca, friends would come to stay with me. My cousin Gail, Hinda from Toronto, Clara from New York, and Sian from South Africa all visited me in Florida. They had very thin hair, and they were unhappy with the way it looked. I would always take my visiting friends to Pompano's Flea Market, which has a wig salon. I suggested that they try one on. They each purchased a wig, and it changed their lives for the better. Hair does make a tremendous difference in how a woman feels. Each time one of my friends bought a wig, she was so happy. They said I changed their lives showing them that they could wear wigs, and feel so much better about how they looked.

Hair played a big part in another story where I was able to help someone change her life. Gail, a cousin whom I love with all my heart, lives in Santa Fe, New Mexico. She was visiting in Florida, and I suggested that she stop using her black hair coloring, and try a light brown or blonde color. She agreed, but she wasn't sure. So, we went to the Flea Market, and I suggested that she could try on some light-colored wigs before she changed her hair color. On her next visit, I suggested that we could go to my colorist, who knows how to remove black dye without damaging someone's hair. Stripping the color off, she became a blonde. It's 20 years later, and she is so beautiful as a blonde, and so happy.

Sometimes you are not aware of how you changed someone's life for a long time—in this case, 40 years!

When Alan and I went skiing for the first time, we fell in love with Aspen, so we purchased a furnished, two-bedroom condo in back of Lift One. It was a spectacular apartment, and the view was incredible. It was in the center of Aspen.

When Alan had financial difficulties in the 1970s, we had to sell the apartment. We had purchased it from friends in Denver for $75,000. They left everything there, including the furnishings, and then bought a big house. We sold for $100,000 because Aspen stopped letting people rent out their condos. I heard that it sold later for $500,000 and then $2 million.

We used to go there in the winter and in the spring. One year, we invited a close friend and neighbor to come on a ten-day vacation with us to Aspen. I wanted my friends to experience skiing for the first time, an experience they would love and would never forget. My friend's husband continued to ski every winter for the rest of his 90-year life span. He kept in shape for skiing. It became his passion for 40 years. When he was 90, his daughter asked me how I knew that skiing would change his life for the better. Sometimes, you don't know.

VOLUME II: What I Learned

After I graduated from FIU in 1974 with my social work degree, I started going to workshops and continuing my education with a series of brilliant teachers to obtain my master's degree in 1979. After that, I continued attending—and eventually teaching—workshops for decades.

One of my first workshops was with Virginia Satir, the mother of family therapy. I was fascinated with her teaching. She became my mentor. Virginia was the author of three of the textbooks that I studied for my master's degree in family therapy. I think I read every book she wrote.

Then I worked with Dr. Harry Sloan, who had been a dentist and had given it up to become a teacher of psychosynthesis. He lectured all over the country, and I studied with him for four years when he came to lecture in Miami.

Then, after my father died, the leader of the grief workshop I attended at Temple Beth Am suggested that I look into the values clarification work of Dr. Sidney Simon. I studied with Sid for 15 years, and learned to lead Values Clarification workshops.

To keep my license, I had to attend learning workshops for credit. That is how I met Dr. Harry Sloan. I learned from him how to use psychosynthesis therapy. One year, my close friend, Gwen, asked me if I would like to hold a week-long workshop at my home. Dr. Sloan had asked her if she knew someone! I agreed. I was living alone in my huge house in Kendal. Harry stayed at my home for a week, and

40 people attended each day. Harry taught therapists and students psychosynthesis as a form of therapy. Actually Harry suggested that I attend a workshop in California at Big Sur, at Esalin. Gwen and I went to California together the following summer for two weeks.

Further, from Rabbi Baumgard and Rabbi Kalman Packouz, I learned the insights Judaism offers about human behavior and our relationship to God. I want to take you a little more deeply into the teachings of these perceptive leaders and share the lessons I learned along the way. I was very fortunate to have these teachers:

- Dr. Sidney Simon—I studied and taught with Sid for 15 years in the area of values clarification. He wrote more than 16 books, including *Self-Esteem*.
- Virginia Satir—She was a well-known author and lecturer, the mother and founder of family therapy.
- Harry Sloan—A lecturer and professor, he taught psychosynthesis.
- The beloved rabbis I learned from, including Temple Beth Am's founding Rabbi Baumgard, Aish HaTorah teacher Kalman Packouz, our Rabbi Menachem Smith at the Vi, and many others I have read and studied.

After these sections, the book ends with a selection of sayings and quotations that I hope you will enjoy.

Dr. Sidney B. Simon

My greatest hope for this book is that sharing my journey of personal growth might help others in their effort to grow. It is a long process that doesn't stop until you die, so I am trying to fill my book with the ways I learned to grow personally in hopes of inspiring my family and friends.

One of my greatest teachers on this journey was Dr. Sidney B. Simon.

Some background: Sid Simon was a pioneer in values clarification and head of the Value Realization Institute. He held a PhD in education and served as professor of Humanist Education at the University of Massachusetts. As early as 1956, he was in the forefront of formulating values clarification theory in conjunction with Louis Raths and Merrill Harmin. His many accomplishments include writing more than 16 books and countless articles on many subjects related to values clarification, including values realization strategies and theories, self-esteem, negative criticism work, and much more. His books include *Getting Unstuck: Breaking Through Your Barriers to Change, Values Clarification* written with Howard Kirschenbaum and Leland W. Howe, and *Forgiveness: How to Make Peace with Your Past and Move On With Your Life,* written with his wife, Suzanne Simon.

He explained, "Values realizations is a process. It consists of theories and tools for pushing through our blocks to change, examining who we are in relation to others, establishing priorities, setting goals, making action plans, and learning how to get the support and cooperation we need to live according to our values."

Studying with him, and then becoming a Values Realization trainer myself, gave me tools I could use to help others increase their positive energy. My goal as a trainer was to make people feel that they got something rich and meaningful out of his exercises and workshops.

My father died in 1979, and I went to a grief class at Temple Beth Am. The teacher told me about Sid Simon. In 1980, I started attending his workshops. Sid taught in so many areas, all for the purpose of helping people "explore who we are and what we want to become."

I want to take you through some of those areas, but first—so that you know why this matters so much—I'd like to explain how I learned and grew from working with him. I learned that I had to go deeper into myself, to stop the busyness of always running and doing. I learned that I was using the daily whirlwind to avoid facing my pain. I learned that I needed to consider my own feelings in order to become more able to consider other people's feelings—what they really felt, not what I wanted them to feel. Through values realization, I found I had to quit lying to myself, pretending not to know what I knew.

I had a tendency to hang out in my old patterns, which were familiar even if they were negative. I had to break that habit, and take risks, so new habits could emerge. I had to listen to my heart, trust it, and stop feeling anxious or seeing myself as a victim. I learned to be grateful for who I am.

For years, I couldn't look deeply into parts of myself or my marriage. I was really afraid and, for a long time, I was not ready. I couldn't see my essence. I was in my own prison, but I kept searching, going to school and going to workshops. I kept running from myself until I learned to surrender to my own essence and to ground myself in figuring out what I really needed.

In a chapter in Sid's *Values Clarification* book, writer Gail Cox shared her thoughts after attending one of Sid's Family Unity workshops. She exactly captured how I felt when I first went. I eventually got Alan and Pam to come. Later Robbie came, and he became the song leader at our workshops.

Gail wrote, "I have been determined to get my whole family

involved in the values realization movement ever since I attended my first workshop…The experience of that workshop was almost like a rebirth to me because I really believed Sid was right when he said, 'This is the way people were meant to be.' I left that workshop feeling more alive than I had in years, as if parts of me that had been numbed or deadened by too much of this and too much of that were being tempted and coaxed and encouraged to grow again. I knew that the process of healing had begun in my life, and I wanted it not only for myself, but for the people I love."

As we learned in Sid's workshops, to build your self-esteem, you must accept that it is available to you. You can feel strong and own your power if you are honest with yourself, give up your fears, acknowledge what you know that you may be pretending not to know, and activate your agency.

Sid taught that six conditions are necessary for self-esteem:

1. *Uniqueness*—Appreciate your special qualities.

2. *Connectedness*—You need connection with your family and friends to build a deep sense of belonging.

3. *Models and mentors*—Learn from someone who is doing better than you are.

4. *Choices*—Use your power to make choices for yourself. Consider people you know who make the choices in their life and don't let others chose for them.

5. *Accomplishments*—Realize what you have achieved by practice and persistence. This includes being productive and building a sense of genuine achievement.

6. *Risk-taking*—You have to take risks and face your fear of failure.

Sid taught, "We create, we promote, and we allow everything that happens in our life." With this framework, I thought about what I had allowed in my life, such as spirituality through Judaism, and what I had pursued, particularly learning. Sid believed that the purpose of life is to learn, to see obstacles as stepping stones and problems as opportunities. He once cautioned, "If your gut is not churning, you're not learning."

I had to ask what I was living for—a difficult question—in order to recognize my purpose: I live for sharing whatever my wisdom is with others, hopefully to help them live better.

The path to living better is personal learning and growth based on understanding and living your values. You can achieve this level of growth through processes called Values Clarification and Values Realization—and that is where Sid Simon was the master.

He explained, "Values realization is an eclectic collection of growth processes, based on value clarification, which has been pieced together from many different threads in the human potential movement."

When Sid was training at New York University, he studied under Louis Rath. Until then, he wrote, "I had never been in a class where they put you in a small group so that you could talk to two or three other students about some topic, and then have the professor give you an exercise or strategy to work on it." At the time, Rath was developing values clarification theory, dealing with the understanding that values are something you take action for, something you own and do, not just vague beliefs. In Rath's statement, values clarification boils down to closing "the gap between our creeds and our deeds."

As a professor of Humanistic Education at the University of Massachusetts, Sid emphasized personal growth through values study and overall wellness. He delved into more than 20 different dimensions of wellness—from recreation to nutrition—that people could practice to live more fully. He offered, "specific, prescribed tools which allow people to take their lives into their own hands…and to move forward with a rational, viable scheme that promotes clarity."

When asked what single message he would like to leave with people who read about him, Sid said, "I would like them to take their lives seriously…to really ask, over and over again, am I living my life at the deepest intensity of my values? I want people to be mindful in their eating, mindful in how they plan and use a day, to name just a few areas. There is only one life to live, and to live it less than at this intense values level seems to me to be wasting God's gift for all of us."

On that basis, I will take you through some of Sid's specific, prescribed tools for personal growth. He would often say that he didn't teach values, he taught the valuing process. He made people in his workshops aware that each decision they made drew on their values, so understanding those values made them better prepared to meet life's realities and challenges.

When Sid led a personal growth workshop, he focused on skills, tools and specific strategies people could take home and use. The tenets of his personal growth workshops included:

- Only you can know what is best for you. You have all the wisdom you need. You do know the answer. Listen to your body and respect its wisdom.
- Each of us is doing the best we can at each moment. If we could do better, we would. Allow for people's fear. Allow for your own fear. Angry feelings are usually based on hurt or fear. Spend time finding out what is beneath the anger instead of venting it.
- When in doubt, validate.
- Don't gossip. Don't give others advice or analysis.

The process of helping others clarify their values starts with being open, encouraging someone to think about value-related concerns and to share those thoughts. The second step is to accept their thoughts and opinions non-judgmentally to show that being honest is safe. And the third step is to help people reach clarity by stimulating them to do some additional thinking about how their values inform their life.

The purpose of Sid's workshops was to explore and celebrate yourself, to discover and reaffirm the beauty you have within you and to help others do that, too.

Sid identified the factors that keep people stuck and unable to risk changing. They include:

- **Fear**—Change could cost too much. It's scary. The two biggest fears are I could get hurt and I could hurt others.
- **Lack of self-esteem**—Deep down, a person may believe that he or she doesn't deserve a better life, that it would be selfish to pursue improvement.
- **Foggy understanding**—People often don't know what they really want.
- **Defensiveness**—People tend to defend and justify what they are doing now, whatever it is.
- **Lack of permission**—Many people don't know how to get the cooperation of those around them. They can't make a clear statement about how they feel and what they want.
- **Lack of will**—People need to learn the language of validation. Use the gift of being able to express yourself. Don't let your mouth be a gatekeeper that shuts out growth because you can't articulate the thoughts that validate your feelings and values.
- **Victimizing**—People feel to blame for being stuck.

To get unstuck, try to set priorities. Consider what your bottom line wishes are and weigh them in importance and intensity. Consider where your current choices come from? Are you projecting what someone else would want from you, like your parents or partner? To move ahead, identify the forces impeding you.

It is not always comfortable to leave denial behind, but you can learn to ask brave questions and make brave statements. Responding to an argument by asking the other person what he or she means is a brave question. Ask, "Do you mean _____?" Then, try to interpret their intent until you get three yesses. This requires you and the other person to ask and answer with integrity.

Sid taught that nothing is hopeless, change is always possible, all feelings are acceptable, adaptation is an option, problems are opportunities, and acceptance of a bad situation is the last alternative. You can forgive the other person, but you must also forgive yourself,

Sid urged his workshop students to keep a personal journal of their growth and to be patient. "We won't forget the problem," he said, "We will just postpone the solution."

Values Clarification

To discuss Dr. Simon's teachings on values clarification, I am drawing from his book, *Meeting Yourself Halfway: Values Clarification Strategies for Daily Living* (Argus Communications, Niles, Illinois, 1974). In the dedication, he cited the teachers who most influenced him, including Louis Rath, his first and most profound influence, Howard Kirschenbaum, Merrill Harmin, who was then director of the National Humanistic Education Center, plus the thousands of university students and workshop attendees who "etched their lives into this book."

The traditional pillars of education and religion have not prepared us to choose our personal set of values or to decide when an action is right or wrong in everyday decision making. They have not given us the necessary training or skill to make conscious value decisions. Consequently, many people are confused between right and wrong, between legality and morality, and they experience a discrepancy between what they say and what they do. You must close that gap to validate yourself and achieve self-esteem.

Clarifying your values so you have a compass to steer your life may be one of the most important things you can do in this confusing world. Too often we make important choices on the basis of peer pressure, unthinking submission to authority, or the power of propaganda.

The process of values clarification is not concerned with what your particular values are. That is up to you. Instead, values clarification gives you a method for determining the content and power of your values. Values clarification is a self-audit, an inventory of soul and spirit, a tool to help you decide freely among alternatives, to determine what has meaning to you. Values clarification is part of a much larger humanistic movement. It is much more concerned with the present and the future and less with exploring the past.

Some strategies are designed to help you take an inventory of various aspects of your life, make decisions, and weigh any consequences. Sid Simon's workshops exposed me to clarification strategies that worked like games. They did not have rules or competition; in fact, they were fun.

On my part, I always avoid competition; I have since childhood when I didn't think I was so smart, and I had a lot of negative thoughts about myself. I guess that is why I loved Sid's workshops. I wasn't competing, but I was learning about myself. This helped me gain a sense of identity and self-worth.

Values are vital in the search for answers to the question, "Who am I?" That is what this book is all about, thanks to Sid Simon's training and classes, which I attended for more than 15 years.

I hope whoever reads this book will be willing to search to know who you are, to commit yourself to standing up and being counted. I hope it will help you develop a greater set of values in all you do. You will know what is worth living for and, as Sid said, if need be, what is worth dying for.

Self-Esteem

To find fulfillment, Freud said, you must be able to love, be able to be loved, and be able to find a sense of purpose in your work or daily activities. To begin, ask yourself, what great things have I achieved in the last 12 months? Am I coming close to my potential? Can I decide how much accomplishment is sufficient?

Oddly, the very quest to be perfect, undermines achievement and self-esteem. Perfection is one of the "deadly Ps," along with procrastination (which can breed threats of depression) and paralysis (which can set in if you decide you can never be good enough).

Instead, turn to validation—accepting that you are important, worthwhile and more than good enough—which offers a path to self-esteem. I worked hard on self-esteem, and now I want to share that ability to feel validated, to say to yourself, "I am lovable and capable." Validation is a way of expressing the reasons you appreciate and respect yourself.

I learned to offer examples of why I respect myself, such as, "I respect myself for the way I stay with what I start until it is finished." "I respect myself for having the strength to continue being a loving and caring person." "I respect myself by not becoming bitter and learning to be more accepting." Taking care of yourself is also a form of self-respect.

I learned the language of validation from Sid. To practice it, fill in these phrases about yourself:

I respect you for…
I admire…
I celebrate…
I cherish…
I applaud…
I appreciate…
I like…
I love…

For example, I wrote this for myself:

I respect you for your openness.
I admire the warmth of your giving nature.
I celebrate your ability to help people.
I cherish your encouraging ways.
I applaud your ability to play the piano and lead us in song.
I appreciate your sensitivity.
I like the way you take notes.
I love the way you laugh and sing.

Validating other people helps you celebrate their uniqueness and individuality. And validating yourself helps you accept yourself fully, flaws and all. For instance, I once wrote, "I respect myself for not becoming a bitter person." Such acceptance is important because if people liked themselves, they wouldn't hurt themselves, and they'd take better care of themselves.

In the process of learning from Sid Simon to accept myself, I re-learned that I am lovable and capable. This is a core revelation for anyone. I saw that I was coping with various challenges, working creatively, getting a lot done each day, and being a loving person. I learned to take delight in doing heavy housework, riding a bike, playing tennis, and nurturing other people.

Sid called the forces that sap your self-esteem " vultures." They fly around your head, attack you, dive right at you, and cause suffering and pain. Vultures are self-put downs. However, you can learn to repel the vultures, which tend to show up in six areas where people commonly disrespect themselves: intelligence, appearance, social life, family, creativity, and sexuality. To get rid of vultures, you must first be aware when you insult yourself. Giving yourself validation kills vultures. Each bit of self-praise or acceptance removes their power by plucking out one feather at a time.

You need a deliberate strategy to banish vultures from your life. Begin by trying to become aware of when you are attacking yourself.

Seek insight into your behavior and use that knowledge to change. Insight can come from books, movies or conversations, but it is an essential catalyst for growth.

To banish vultures, do something for yourself. Phrase your self-talk in positive terms. Set goals for new behaviors, including rewards for accomplishing small steps so you feel your successes. To get rid of a vulture, replace it with a nourishing message. Tell yourself, "I am lovable and capable."

Dr. Simon offered a two-step plan for change: First, find behavioral alternatives to use instead of putting yourself down. Look for authentic, comfortable substitutes and options to replace negative self-messages. Be open to seeing yourself positively. Such changes should start flamboyantly and immediately with no exceptions to the new behavior, no cheating. Sometimes the best way to institute change is to work with a partner and even sign a contract. Ask yourself what commitments you are willing to make, what plan you could follow, how can you avoid sabotaging yourself, and how will you reward yourself to celebrate your success.

Second, nourish change so it can develop. That means finding support, respect, and validation from others, as well as from within yourself. Sometimes that help will be reciprocal—when people help you, be prepared to give back to them.

In Sid Simon's workshops, we used a variety of exercises to help people build self-esteem. Here are a few you can consider:

- Make a list of the three best, most productive or most successful years of your life, and identify what went right.

- Make a list of your goals, identifying achievements that would bring you power, connection, uniqueness, and the other necessary elements of self-esteem. To make your list real, outline the steps you would need to take to fulfill these goals. Assign a time frame to each step. What do you need to do this week, this month, in three months, and so on.

- Number a page from 1 to 50, and answer the question, Who Am I? by listing 50 words that describe you or what you want to do. My initial list included, “Scared, mother, giving, lover, sensitive, grateful, lonely, happy, social worker, woman, housekeeper, laundress, tennis player, giver, flexible, rigid, learner, need new experiences, creative, organizer…” Just let it flow.

If I could identify Sid’s core teaching about self-esteem it would be: We must love ourselves before we can love another person, and that requires validating ourselves. *Loving yourself is the foundation of a strong, positive self-concept.*

Relationships

The basic dynamics hampering personal relationships rest on those two big fears: the fear of getting hurt (again) and the fear of hurting someone else. Overcoming these core fears requires taking a few specific actions:

- Validate your self-esteem.
- Try to understand the other person’s logic.
- Develop alternative approaches.
- Define what areas are the other person’s problems (maybe he or she had bad parents?) and what areas are your problems.
- Try to see their point of view.
- Ask if the mix is wrong. Perhaps your styles of loving are imbalanced. Can you address the imbalance? Do you need to state a clear yes or no more often? Sources of conflict that can cause an imbalance include family, friends, work, love, sex, death, politics, finances, and areas of responsibility. Ask yourself where you have the flexibility to redress the imbalance.

- Avail yourself of some counseling or have some therapeutic outlet.
- Use your sense of humor, so you don't take yourself too seriously.
- Build on your strong spiritual values.
- Pay attention to your overall wellness.

In Sid's workshops I learned a set of "Relationship Principles" written by Georgia and Shaw Noble that can help you navigate this crucial area. These tenets sound difficult to practice, but they are healthier than hating someone. Clinging to hatred sets you up to be disappointed and leaves you hanging onto old viewpoints. Use these principles to create a better atmosphere for working things out or making pro or con decisions about a relationship. They are:

- The experience of love and satisfaction can be mine—This is true whenever you decide and is always possible at any time and any place and in any circumstances.
- I alone solely generate the experience of that love—You create, promote, allow, and abet whatever happens in your relationships. This is true of both the delightful and the problematic parts of a relationship. If you find yourself judging or blaming, see these emotions as forms of resisting the relationship. Realize that trying to get someone else to change is like standing in front of a wall and commanding it to change. The only way you can get another person to change is to first change yourself, and thereby change your reactions to the other person.
- My intimate relationships are my opportunity to express myself as a lover—How or whether you do this is a function of your willingness to express love, and it does not depend on how others behave.
- The other people in my life love me—That is unquestioned and not negotiable. So, whatever the circumstances and whatever the

feelings or the words they say or the actions they take, assume that the behaviors which involve you are the behaviors of people who love you, even though it doesn't look like that at the time.

- Whatever the circumstances (delightful or troubling), I will operate as though I'm the cause of it, and the other person is doing exactly what I got him or her to do—Try to maintain that assumption even when it seems impossible that you could have caused the other person's behaviors. I learned that we create, promote, and allow everything that happens in our lives, but this can be very hard to grapple with and to accept.
- My relationships work perfectly for me and the people involved with me. Everything that happens is a manifestation that I am loved.

Sid Simon's teaching about relationships were grounded in values and honesty.

If you are having difficulties in your love relationship, ask what benefits you are getting from it. Perhaps you feel cared about, you're not alone, you are growing, you see the other half of yourself, you are loved, you feel secure, you have someone you can count on, you get feedback and a trustworthy second opinion, you have support, you have companionship, and you feel bonded. In evaluating these benefits—or their absence—ask if you know what you can change and if you can accept what you cannot change.

The factors that help a relationship include communication, loverlike behavior, willingness to work on the relationship, flexibility, openness, self-esteem, physical affection, autonomy, honesty and listening to one another. In comparison, the factors that hurt a relationship include refusing to accept communication, selfishness, being a doormat, giving up, allowing no choices, being inflexible, lacking self-esteem, and lacking touch (or skin hunger), which leads to a deficit of personal nourishment.

Touching is part of feeding relationship. Consider who physically touched you—positively—when you were a child, like your parents and relatives. Such skin nourishment helps personal growth. It feels good. We never outgrow our need for it. Non-sexual touching is part of basic communication. Touch builds trust, or at least it did before Covid. It will be interesting to see what researchers in this area learn in the wake of the pandemic.

Jealousy also can badly undermine a relationship, but you can deal with it more effectively if you understand how it works. The events that can provoke someone to feel jealous can include the other person doing something unilaterally without consultation, personal feelings of inadequacy, something unfair happening, feeling a sexual threat, and giving in to thoughts of retribution. Avoid arousing jealousy in your partner by communicating your feelings, being honest and straightforward, being aware and open to your partner, and trying not to be in relationship or situations that have different values than you do.

Obviously communication is critical. If you and those with whom you are trying to maintain a relationship can avoid the most notable roadblocks to communication, you may be able to arrive at a smoother path. Sid Simon identified these roadblocks which, in one way or another, communicate non-acceptance:

1. **Ordering, directing, commanding**—Telling or ordering the other person to do something communicates that his or her needs don't matter. These messages engender feelings of resentment or anger, frequently causing the other person to express hostility, fight back, or test your will.

2. **Warning, admonishing, threatening**—Telling someone what consequences will occur if he or she does or doesn't do what you say can make that person feel fearful and submissive. These messages communicate your lack of respect for the other person's needs or wishes. They also invite him or her to test your firmness, to do something you have warned against just to see if the consequences you promise actually happen.

3. **Moralizing, preaching, obliging**—Giving someone orders brings to bear the power of external authority, duty or obligation. They make people feel that you do not trust their judgment.

4. **Advising, giving suggestions or solutions**—Telling someone how to solve his or her own problems can cause that person to become dependent on you or to feel that you haven't understood their situation at all. This includes statements like, "You can kick the smoking habit if you just try harder."

5. **Persuading with logic, arguing, instructing, lecturing**—Trying to influence the other person with facts or your opinions makes it seem that you see him or her as inadequate, subordinate or inferior. People seldom like to be shown that they are wrong. Logic and facts can make another person defensive and resentful.

6. **Judging, criticizing, disagreeing, blaming**—Negative judgments convey a message that the other person is stupid, unworthy, or bad. As you judge someone, he or she may judge themselves in the same way. Harsh evaluations strongly influence people to keep their feelings to themselves and never share them with you. The only message more devastating than negative evaluation is frequent negative evaluation.

7. **Praising, agreeing, evaluating positively**—Contrary to the idea that praise is always beneficial to the recipient, it often has a negative effect, particularly if it does not fit the other person's self-image. Praise is often seen as manipulative. It can embarrass people if spoken in public or, conversely, make them need constant approval in order to function.

8. **Name-calling, ridiculing, shaming**—Making another person feel foolish, stereotyping, or categorizing him or her has a devastating effect on self-image. It can make people feel unworthy and unloved.

9. **Interpreting, analyzing, diagnosing**—Telling someone what his or her motives are, or analyzing why he or she is doing or saying something,

communicates that you have him or her figured out or diagnosed. The message, "I can see through you" tends to cut off communication and to teach the other person not to share his or her feelings.

10. **Reassuring, sympathizing, consoling, supporting**—Trying to make the other person feel better, talking him or her out of his or her feelings, or trying to make those feelings go away is not as helpful as most people think. Discounting or sympathizing often stops further communication. Reassuring people who feel disturbed may simply convince them that you don't understand and just want them to stop feeling how they feel.

11. **Probing, questioning, interrogating**—Searching for more information to help you solve the problem may simply convey your lack of trust in the other person. People often feel threatened by questions, and each question limits their freedom to talk about what they want to discuss. In a sense, each question dictates his or her next message. Interrogating the way someone communicates with you is not a good method of facilitating their ability to solve problems.

12. **Withdrawing, distracting, humoring**—Trying to get the other person away from the problem means pushing it aside, not solving it. That may make the person feel rejected. People are generally serious and intent when they need to talk about something difficult, but when you respond with kidding, you make them feel belittled or hurt.

Instead of blocking communication, facilitate it with active listening. Offer silence, nods, and other signals of acceptance to encourage people to communicate what they feel.

The Sense of Forgiveness

The secret of my life is to gather the nourishments, insights, and wisdom to change, and to learn to forgive. Sid Simon laid out very helpful information about how forgiveness works and how you can use it to release yourself and others from pain. Consider five issues:

1. **To be able to see the warts, weaknesses, and all**—Be aware that you can't allow people to abuse you under the guise of knowing you will forgive them, but you can evaluate a situation and a person candidly and decide to forgive.

2. **To not pretend not to know**—You can't put your head in the sand or assign qualities to another person that he or she does not have.

3. **You did the best you could**—Forgiveness starts, if you can do it authentically, with you saying three times to your parent, partner, or whoever you want to forgive: "I know you did the best you could. I know you did the best you could. I know you did the best you could." Until we can forgive our parents and accept that they did all they could with what they knew at the time, we may not be able to forgive ourselves.

4. If you had had more insight into your life or more nourishment in your life, you would have done better.

5. Seek wisdom so you don't have to repeat what your parents (or anyone else) did.

Sid did a specific workshop in which he outlined a three-stage process to explain how forgiveness works. This speaks in particular to adults who were mistreated as children, but it is broadly applicable.

The first stage of the forgiveness process is Denial.

To work on forgiveness, you may have to deal with memories you have blocked out. You must not minimize whatever happened to you. You may be pushing down your feelings when you make excuses like, "It wasn't that bad" or "It was a long time ago." For some people, the payoff for denying past problems, like abuse, is that confronting how they were treated makes them feel damaged or guilty. Tell yourself you are entitled to set that aside, that, "I've had enough pain now." Don't let it block your joy. Reclaim your energy.

The second stage of the forgiveness process is Self-Blame.

You may have left denial behind, but now you hold yourself accountable, even though people may have harmed you when you were a child who had no personal agency at all. Self-messages like it was my fault, I set it up, I asked for it, I colluded in it, I didn't stop it, or if only I had…all amount to feeling like these bad events were due to something about you as an individual, something you did. Instead, try to see these events from the point of view of the person or people who hurt you. Why did they act that way?

To address the issue of self-blame, Sid Simon's workshop students carried out a helpful, but difficult, exercise from therapist Ira Progroff: Write a letter to yourself from the person who hurt you. In the letter, have that person explain his or her viewpoint, take responsibility for the harm he or she did, and apologize in their voice to you.

Here is the letter I wrote to myself as if it were from my ex-husband and in his voice:

Dear Esther,
I'm sorry for what I did to you when I left. I was running away from myself. I wasn't aware of anything as far as you were concerned. I was angry and hurt and couldn't stop drinking or blaming. It was easier to blame you than to take responsibility for myself.

I destroyed myself and destroyed everyone in my family—you especially. You were easy. You never fought back. I lost everything—business, friends, family, my integrity. My new wife really wanted me. I listened to everything she said. I thought she would save me from

> *myself, and she tried being a mother. I'm sorry for how I kept our children on my side, blaming you always. I really was blaming my mother, who I hated and was terrified of. I repeated the same behavior my crazy mother inflicted on me when she and my father divorced.*
>
> *I now know that maybe I was cruel to you, but remember I never could face my feelings so I just kept drinking and denying everything. We have wonderful children, and thanks to you for that! Please forgive me. I now feel grateful to you for the wonderful, kind, caring, and giving mother and wife you were.*

Now, please understand that is what I wish he had said—he didn't say it, but articulating that message helped me. It is important to think through why the people who hurt you acted as they did so that you can move out of the stage of blaming yourself.

In fact, you cannot skip a stage in the forgiveness process. You must fully experience each step until someone in the chain breaks the cycle, probably you—since you're doing the work.

The third stage of the forgiveness process is being a Victim.

Victims beget victims, so you do not want to be one. Sid offered tools that help people who felt like victims reclaim their personal power. Victims have a "poor me" attitude. They complain. Victims feel powerless and in pain. That is the doorway out: pay attention to the hurt you feel and seek comfort from the pain.

Victimhood manifests in three variations. First is the whiner who mourns and sighs, becomes a workaholic, and treats life as a pity party. The second is the mean victim who is filled with anger, puts other people down, and acts like a wounded animal who attacks everyone in reach. The third is the self-indulger who tries somehow to get rid of pain, often with drugs or alcohol or overeating. I would eat a half-gallon of M&M ice cream and cookies as my answer to having been hurt as a child. The self-indulger often is committing systematic suicide by destroying his or her own body.

Victims call attention to their pain and manifest it. Sometimes they take on the role of being a victim for so long because it gives them excuses based on how much they hurt. To recover—and to forgive—the victim must want life and must reach for the opposite forces, such as eating good nutritious food instead of over-indulging. In that sense, you can turn to several others activities as the opposites of systematic suicide. Start with life-affirming nutrition, physical exercise, and overall wellness.

Try to develop a loving relationship that includes taking one day each week for the two of you to do things you enjoy together. Every six months, take a week.

To develop such a relationship—and even to eat healthfully or exercise—you have to want life and to make that desire actual based on your actions.

The fourth stage of the forgiveness process is Indignation

Indignation is righteous, justified anger, though it doesn't have to be violent or even loud. It's a signal to make a change. Anger can take on many faces, including fear, guilt, shame, embarrassment, grief and frustration, but its primary emotion is hurt.

Anger holds an important place in the journey of healing. Again, a self-revelatory piece of communication can help you express your anger and put it in perspective. You can write a telegram to yourself to do something about your anger. This was my message to myself:

> *Dear Esther,*
> *Express how you feel. Don't suppress it. Allow yourself to be angry. Find out where its coming from. It rests in your expectations of another person. Don't accept responsibility for anyone else's anger. Don't get sucked into it. People will try to blame you for their own anger. Don't allow it. Say what's bother you. Take responsibility for your behavior.*

I learned from Sid Simon to seek the benefit in your anger. Express it to the person you feel caused it. Ask for what you need. Use that anger to motivate change. Get that energy out. Love yourself.

The fifth stage of the forgiveness process is being a Survivor

Be proud that you made it. You are here! Celebrate what you learned from all that pain. I know I struggled to do the best I could. If I had had more insight, I would have done better, or if I had had more nourishment in my life, I would have been able to cope better. I struggled in my marriage to do the best I could, given my support system, and now I have survived and rebuilt my life. When you reach this stage in the forgiveness process, you are a victor, and you can have some laughter and humor. It is still valid to say, "I did the best I could." That is always valid.

The fifth stage of the forgiveness process is Integration

This is the period in your forgiveness process of making sense of the whole experience. You integrate what happened along the way, acknowledge that it did happen to you, but it is not you. Tell yourself, I am more than it. We can also come to believe that the person who hurt us is more than the hurt they did to us.

We all have the ability to experience pain and hurt and to give pain and hurt. It is okay to look back, but don't stare. You want to be moving on, not hanging on. As you will see, going through the process of forgiveness is important, but isn't easy. However, refusing to go through it keeps you in an emotional prison. As Sid taught, it takes a hell of a lot of energy to keep rejecting someone. Consider what that is doing to you. Instead, take the road to healing and wholeness.

Integration is about becoming yourself. To bring about your integration, it may help to write—for your own benefit—a letter to the person you need to forgive. This was my letter:

Dear Alan,
I am on a healing journey, and this is where I am with you. I must forget to be angry and blame you. I'm on a road past that stage. I'm not going to live in the past. I'm living in the present. I can't change the past, and I can't live in the future while hating you for not being someone you were not able to be or for the disappointment of my expectations of how you should have behaved.

You did the best you could coming from the family you came from. Your father died when you were six years old, and your mother was divorced three times.

I am on this healing journey, and it's time for me to express to our children that I have the ability to forgive you. You did the best you could. What good would it serve me to be bitter and resent you now. I am not a victim. I am an integrated whole human being working toward my overall wellness. I am grateful to have my wonderful, supportive children and friends. I realize that my integration is about me, not about you. It's about being me.

The process of forgiveness led me to a personal turning point. I had worked through my fears and done something about them, so that I could get unstuck. Otherwise, I would have stayed stuck. This enabled me to think about what I wanted to do with the rest of my life, after my divorce. I could think about the relationships I wanted to build with my children and even to think about a future loving relationship with a man.

To mark such turning points, consider writing a letter to a transitional event, not a person, but an event. Reflect on what it taught you, what it gave you, and how your life would be different if it hadn't happened.

I wrote this letter to my divorce:

Dear Divorce,
Now that you've finally happened, I'm so grateful. You're what I've been waiting for, I think, for 30 years. I feel so fortunate to have

this opportunity to start a new life when anything I want to do—or be—is up to me. It's hard to believe I deserve this chance to find happiness and peace within myself and with whoever I chose to share my life with.

I don't know what's ahead really, but I'm not afraid to search for happiness in the future. I'm grateful for the years behind me that gave me my children and the life's experiences that brought me to you. Divorce, you were an uphill turning point for me. It took three years of separation for me to make the transition from being a married woman of 27 years to being a single woman. It was a terrible struggle.

Now that you've happened, this turning point has made me feel light, independent, and connected. I am grounded from having gone through this crisis. I am still growing into the kind of person I choose to be—happy and peaceful.

Of all the attitudes we can take, the greatest is the attitude of gratitude. I learned through Sid Simon's workshops, to think about what's going on inside you. I'm grateful that I have let go of anger, that I've learned what I really want, that I could get divorced—because I think I would have died of heartbreak otherwise.

I appreciate that I have grown. Forgiveness brought me to gratitude, which is a celebration of life. At the end of the forgiveness process, there is one more assignment: Write a letter of gratitude to someone involved in a turning point in your life. So, of course, I wrote to my ex-husband. Though I never sent the letter—and he has since passed away—it encapsulates lessons I learned, and it starts and ends with being grateful:

Dear Alan,

I must write this letter of gratitude to you now that we are divorced. It is something I have wanted to tell you for the three years of our separation. I was so young and naive when we married. I knew something was wrong the evening of our wedding, but I didn't understand what I was feeling. You tried so hard to keep your secret, and you achieved that for a long time. I was so busy being defensive and not feeling like a worthwhile person while raising three beautiful, healthy children.

I thought I was the problem. I believed something was wrong with me. I started to see a psychologist. He helped me live with this burden, but I still didn't see the real problem: your alcoholism and your inability to give love, And, I didn't even know it. No, I knew it, but I wouldn't admit to it. Instead, I tried to change you. For 27 years, I really believed if I showed you another way, you would change. The years weren't wasted. You did the best you could. The children were the gifts of God.

I'm so grateful to you for your ability to achieve financially and to make sure our family had no financial problems. I had so much. I'm grateful now, and the children's love through the years made it bearable. Your drinking problems were your secret. And you blamed me instead of taking the responsibility of trying to do something about it. I couldn't accept you as you were, and I spent our marriage trying to change you. Now I am grateful to you for all you did do, and grateful to be whole and at peace.

I have learned that we have to forgive ourselves before we forgive others. We have to love ourselves before we can love another person. It all starts with reaching our inner higher power, which is God and our connection to God. We need to have faith that He is always with us. We may lose our faith swimming in the river of life, but we can always connect and reach for the God within us, not only by changing other people's lives, but by changing our own lives through God's teaching.

Overall Wellness

In his book *Values Clarification*, which I will quote extensively in this section, Sid explained the importance of the dimensions of overall wellness, the factors that are necessary to keep you physically and mentally healthy. They are:

One: Alone Time

"All of us need alone time, but most of us are so frightened by the silence of being alone that we try to get as little of it as we can. Yet for overall wellness, we all need at least some time each day to be alone. It is time to be used for prayer, or meditation, or daydreaming, or thinking. It must be silent, peaceful and solitary. Almost no one gets this alone time, but it is important. If you can build alone time into your life, you'll be making an investment in your overall wellness. It is the place to begin. Try to make a decision right now: When will you schedule your alone time?" Early in the morning? After work? Before bed? Make a choice and with that choice start the overall wellness program in your life."

Two: Improved Nutrition

"There is no way overall wellness can operate in your life without substantial change in what you do with your mouth. The mouth is the last gatekeeper over which we have total physical (if not psychological) control. We can let some things in and keep some things out. Improving our nutrition involves taking control of that gate, stopping the bad things from going in," and changing the balance of what we eat to favor consuming good things.

There are some enormously challenging choices for you to make on the road to wellness. You can start by eliminating salt and sugar as well as over processed foods and, when you can, caffeine and high cholesterol foods, including red meat.

As Sid wrote, "I am not for taking all the joy out of your life. I'm arguing that there are sweeter and richer joys in life. If the only pleasure in your life comes through your mouth, then you have significant work to do in locating where joy really is."

Other changes in your routine can help you attain wellness. "Stay out of fast-food traps, try not to eat anything after 7:00 PM, and that includes nothing while watching television. Remember what Richard Simmons said, 'Food you eat after 7:00 PM is like a mistress. It goes right to bed with you.'"

Three: A Counseling Outlet

"Alcoholics Anonymous has taught all of us that we don't have to go it alone." In fact, Sid argues that each person needs a reliable, available counseling outlet. This can be a friend or a professional therapist "who has worked with you before and is always there for a catch up session… The main function of a therapist is to help a person regain courage, and this is best done with the process of encouragement, helping them tap back into their strengths and inherent wisdom."

Four: An Exercise Program

Develop a regular, consistent exercise routine that covers three crucial factors: aerobics, strength building, and flexibility and stretching. Select something you enjoy doing—swimming, dancing, brisk walking—so that you will stay with it. "There are dozens of possibilities… but one thing is clear: You need a cardio-vascular system that will be around to support you in your zest for life."

Five: Maintain a Juicy Love Relationship

"I imagine one could have overall wellness as a monk, but I am not a monk," Sid wrote, "and in my non-celestial life, I know I need love. Building and maintaining a juicy love relationship is high on my list of overall wellness dimensions, for all the sweet advantages a good love in my life brings. The advantages of holding and being held, of snuggling and being snuggled. The therapeutic benefits of having someone to tell your day to. The delight of making plans with someone, of sharing trials, and celebrating holidays, and practicing rituals and ceremonies together. If you have been there, you know it. If you haven't been there then you need to get there, maybe again."

If you are seeking a new love relationship, plan for it. Create a planning board with a list of the traits you are looking for, and rank them in importance to you. My list included integrity, honesty, ambition, loving children, being validating, having social skills, being sensuous and having chemistry, and being free of addiction. I also listed clear communication, intellectual stimulation, spirituality and emotional accessibility as important to me. Try to define what's important to you, for instance, I realized that to me having plenty of time together was more important than having plenty of money.

As you create this planning board, look back on your love life and see if you can detect patterns you may want to repeat or avoid. Try making a list of people you have fallen in love with, how long your relationship lasted, who ended it, who loved more, what impact it had on you, and what elements you would want to repeat—or not repeat —in a future relationship. Each relationship is a building block in how you see love, and it provides information you can use to build future relationships. Ask yourself what you need to do to get more love in your life. Are you staying too busy or limiting yourself in ways that block new relationships?

Six: Being Part of a Solid Support Group

Research into burnout prevention says that "the single most important thing you can do to prevent burnout is to be part of reliable, adequate, and active support group…A support group isn't just a bunch of guys who get together to play poker. That has some advantages, but it isn't what a support group really needs to do. A genuine support group meets regularly every three to four weeks and in that meeting…talks about some personal things, but mostly about professional things. It's a forum for seeking specific help on specific problems, for trying out new ideas, and for getting new ideas."

When I attended an Explorations Institute in 1976, I learned how much you can benefit from a group experience. I learned how to communicate in the here and now, to focus on awareness, and to explore the world of inner feelings. In the right group, you can get honest feedback on how you come across so that you can see yourself as others see you. Also, you can learn to be more honest with those around you in the safe atmosphere of a supportive group. I learned to become more sensitive to the ways people communicate and the powerful messages they transmit nonverbally with facial expressions, posture, body language, and tone of voice.

In this kind of group I learned how to be close to other people while still respecting my freedom to assert myself. Such a group provides a setting for experimenting with new ways of relating to others beyond just two or three close friends. A group is a little like a laboratory where you can try out all kinds of experiences, and you can risk new ways of relating and communicating.

A support group should offer friendship and comfort. It fosters respect, compassion, safety, insight and personal growth. A support group should have these intentions: to maintain positive feelings, to nurture and support, to provide connectedness and a sense of belonging, to develop strategies for living, to help people grow in an atmosphere of trust and confidentiality, and to build relationships. In the right group, you can find mentors and models, be taken seriously, get new ideas, and find focused time and attention for brainstorming and solving problems together.

Seven: Time Management

In Sid's words: "Now we come to a big dimension of overall wellness: making time for the six dimensions of overall wellness we've already discussed. Basic good time management is hard-nosed goal setting." It depends on getting your priorities straight. "Get your act together now and decide what you really want to do with the rest of your life. Where do you want to be 10 years from now? Read a good time management book, or several. Sid liked Alan Lakein's *How to get Control of Your Time and Your Life* (the used paperback is still available on Amazon for $6). Lakein said that you should, "never touch a piece of paper more than once." Sid added, "If you don't have time to deal with it, don't read it." That is a good start for time management.

Sid always advised us that "none of the dimensions of overall wellness are insurmountable. They do require priority setting in your total life, some hard-nosed decision making and getting clear on your values."

Eight: Know What You Really Value

Check out a good book on values clarification and do some of its exercises to begin to define what you really want. "To live a life without clear values is to end up wishy-washy, ambivalent, indecisive, and frequently depressed. A life steered by the values shines; it is productive, purposeful and full of zest," Sid wrote. People pay a personal penalty for postponing or denying the need to gain clarity about what they value.

Create an inventory of things you could do more of that lift you out of the blues, like being with people or calling a friend, working with plants, making art or music, getting some recreation, or planning—or taking—a trip. Be ready to take steps to renew your spirits and boost your energy.

Nine: Increase the risk in your life

"You can't have overall wellness without abundant risk in your life. Risk is an anomaly. We've been taught to seek security and safety. We try to get predictability in our lives. What we end up with is rigidity and tiny dreams. A life without risk is like a flat road that stretches interminably into a not very exciting landscape.

"Bruce Larson writes about risk in his book *The Meaning and Mystery of Being Human* (also available used on Amazon, for $6.47). Larson implies that risk-taking may well be the most important factor in preventing mental illness or promoting mental health."

Larson outlines four different kinds of risk taking—intellectual, spiritual, physical and emotional—that can help you build wisdom and skill. An intellectual risk can involve learning something you don't know. A spiritual risk can mean finding your God or sense of a higher power. A physical risk could involve facing some danger, like learning to ski, and feeling that sense of exhilaration. And an emotional risk usually comes down to intimacy. The greatest risks, as discussed, may come from the fear of being hurt or of hurting someone else. And the very biggest risk is going back in again after being hurt or hurting someone else. Risk takes courage, but it is crucial to your mental health and to learning what you really want.

Risk also arises when you allow yourself to evaluate what you have created, promoted, and allowed in your life. I learned that we promote, allow, and create everything in our lives. This is very difficult to accept. As with some other lessons, you won't like everything you learn, but you will grow from knowing it.

Ten: Being Open to Change

"We cling to things that are familiar, even though they may be part of our systematic suicide," Sid wrote. People tend to resist change, even change that is ultimately very good for them, like quitting smoking. Yet, each of the crucial steps to overall wellness requires you to make some change.

Consider this exercise: Create five columns next to this list of the ten components of overall wellness.

THE 10 COMPONENTS	**1**	**2**	**3**	**4**	**5**
1. Alone time					
2. Improve nutrition					
3. A counseling outlet					
4. Exercise					
5. A love relationship					
6. A support group					
7. Time management					
8. Knowing what you value					
9. Taking risks					
10. Being open to change					

In the **first column**, check the items you are doing right now.

In the **second column**, give yourself a rating on a scale of 1 to 10 about how adequately you are doing each of these ten things right now (10 is highest).

In the **third column**, put down the initials of someone who could help you or support you in getting better at each individual wellness dimension.

In the **fourth column**, rank the ten dimensions in order of the ones which would most contribute to your overall wellness life. Include all ten.

In the **fifth column**, make a plan of which of these steps you want to improve first, second, and so forth.

Negativity works against wellness, as writer Jack Osman explains in Sid's *Values Clarification* book. In fact, negativity is the opposite of wellness, he writes. "Negativity tends to be self-defeating...and counterproductive.

"Wellness implies that self-responsibility can make a difference, that you can be in control through personal, positive action or thinking. Optimism is implicit within wellness. One negative experience leads to another, and soon the person is consumed by…negativity. Criticism of others, the system, and the self will follow. Hope and optimism drop out of the critic's vocabulary. Extended interactions with people consumed by negativity can be toxic. Their poison contaminates us. Sometimes, we need to limit our interactions with such people through 'creative neglect.'"

In his very productive conversation about negative criticism, Osman cites Sid Simon's book on the subject. Osman explains, "Criticism is analogous to someone stabbing our chest cavity with a sharp knife—it drains our life force, our vitality, our energy. Few people handle criticism graciously on the inside. Yet, we've been 'taught' that criticism is good for us. It's necessary. It will help us grow. It will make you strong. (Who among us really believes that?)

In Sid's book, *Negative Criticism*, he asks readers if they can recall an instance of criticism that genuinely led to personal growth or made a meaningful difference. People can cite very few examples of genuinely productive critique. Instead, Osman writes, "Nearly all criticisms have an air of negativity. In a sense, they are put downs that are often destructive of one's self concept, image, and acceptance.

"What we do learn from the collective criticisms that we've received is the art of giving criticism. We become experts at criticizing others. We also learn to criticize ourselves. We work against our best interests and put ourselves down. Depression—staying down—often follows.

Osman finds there is no such thing as "constructive criticism?" "Constructive criticism may well be a euphemism, a guise for negative criticism. Constructive criticism still hurts…Criticism, constructive or destructive, is a subtle form of manipulation or shaping of another person's thinking or behavior. Underneath most criticism can be found a comment like: 'You are different than me. You would be better off if you did things my way'."

Osman says to scrutinize any criticism you plan to deliver by evaluating how you'd respond to four questions summed up in the acronym NETS:

1. "Is the criticism Necessary?

2. Is it Edifying? Does it help the person grow?

3. Is it Truth-full?

4. Is it Self-serving? Does it really help you more than them?"

Realize that people are fragile, and criticism can leave lasting scars. Before you issue negative criticism, ask yourself if the person is in any shape or position to hear it. Is it something they've heard many times before? That's nagging. Can they do something about it? Are you committed to picking up the pieces after you take someone apart? Is there any item in what you plan to criticize that is a projection of your own history or behavior?

I learned that the traits I dislike in other people are the things I can't stand when I do them myself. Empathy is the path to avoiding projecting your stuff onto someone else. Try to put yourself in the other person's shoes. Be aware of what kind of people annoy you, and try to view them with compassion. I learned that I am more likely to have a negative reaction to people who are negative themselves, and I want to be with people who are positive and accomplish things.

Teacher supervisor Mayme Porter said that in evaluating a teacher, she asks three questions instead of criticizing. She asks: "What did you like about what you did? If you could do it over, what would you do differently?" And, "what help do you need from me?" Sid often warned his workshop participants to avoid having a "red pencil mentality" that sought other people's mistakes. Instead of seeing what's wrong with someone, try to look at them with empathy as a human being. See if you can validate them instead.

Realize, as Osman writes, that the "double-edged sword of criticism infects the receiver of the criticism and re-infects the sender. More dominos of negativity continue to fall into one another, and before we know it, we're caught in a web of negativity and pessimism.

"Persons concerned about wellness would be wise to filter criticism through NETS to avoid getting trapped in a web of negativity. Ask: How is that criticism helping someone's personal or professional growth? Try to counterbalance each criticism with a validation—a genuine statement about the person's beauty or worth."

"When knives of criticism are thrown your way, take responsibility, and protect your level of emotional wellness...Repeat the following quote as a rhythmic chant until you believe it: '*No matter what you say about me, I'm still a worthwhile person.*' Remember that quote the next time you have a fight with your lover or get a not-so-positive year end evaluation. When you can sincerely protect yourself from those who desire to put you down, you have taken a positive step toward your personal wellness."

In an essay cited at Sid's workshops, writer Bill Borcherdt, ACSW, offers some tools you can use if you're the target of someone's constant negative criticism, or of that person's irritability and impatience. You can't change how someone else behaves, but you can extend some influence and, to a point, "teach people how to respond" to you by the way you react to them.

Try Borcherdt's eight strategies with your constant critic:

1. *Don't blame yourself*—You're not responsible for someone else's rigid disapproval.

2. *Don't blame the other person either*—The critic's stream of rebuke says a lot more about him or her than about you. As Borcherdt writes, "he's mad because he's thin-skinned and has no sense of perspective. To continue to blame him only reinforces his inclinations to get down on himself. The less upset you get, and the less of an audience you give him, the sooner he is likely to un-upset himself."

3. *Accept the situation as it is*—It exists. You may not like it, but you can't wish it away.

4. *Set the limits of compromise or conditions of the relationship*—You can set boundaries without being argumentative. "How you say something is as important as what you say. There is a difference between telling someone how you feel and telling them off." To set a boundary, start with "I," as in, "I would like to discuss a concern…"

5. *Help the other person*—A negative person is in emotional pain. Try to be sincerely empathetic and understanding. Borcherdt suggests saying something like, "It sounds like you were really given a hard time today, is there anything I can do to help?"

6. *Don't rescue*—That means, don't finish your critic's sentences, ease him or her over rough spots, or otherwise enable your critic. Step back.

Decide you won't own his or her problems, but a solution for that sourness is out there somewhere, and perhaps you can help find it.

7. *Become more self-interested*—Having one critic in your life doesn't have to make your whole life sad. Go after things you enjoy. Then you'll be in a good mood, and that might be contagious.
8. *Show the critic that it's in his or her best interest to change*—Model positivity. In time, your patience and refusal to rise to the bait can demonstrate a more productive approach.

Your attitude may or may not influence your critic to change, but you will feel a lot better.

Burnout

Louise Continelli wrote an excellent article based on Sid's work on preventing burnout. She tracks the signs of burnout, and then tells you how to prevent it.

You are at risk of burnout, she writes, if you give up, quit trying, and feel sorry for yourself. You may be burning out if you eat, smoke, or drink to excess, and you just don't have the energy to figure out how to restore your sense of wellbeing.

One step to take is to get rid of toxic people in your life. Be confident that you deserve better relationships. Don't listen to selfish demands, put downs, or emotional destructiveness. Instead of feeling defensive about the status quo, move in a more positive direction.

Try to associate with nourishing relatives, colleagues or friends who listen without judgment, encourage you, and reveal themselves without fear. As you learn to define what really matters to you (values clarification), you will be more able to embrace total wellness and recharge your energy. Sid Simon's formula for fighting against burning out parallels his overall wellness agenda. He lists these steps you can take to prevent burnout:

1. Improved nutrition. That's mouth work. What you eat reflects your values.
2. Exercise to live longer and to stay healthy. Find your sport and go for it!
3. Take regular alone time for meditation or prayer.
4. Take risks in the four areas Larson discusses: physical, emotional, spiritual and intellectual.
5. Build an adequate support group.
6. Get rid of toxic people.
7. Get some recreation, perhaps including learning some skill for personal growth and tranquility, like needlepoint or woodwork. This is literally re-creation, something that re-creates you.
8. Know what you really, really love (values).
9. Find or maintain a love relationship.
10. Restore physical touch in your life.
11. Manage your time.
12. Find a counseling outlet.
13. Seek a maximum of validation and a minimum of negative criticism.
14. Be open to change.
15. Have fun in your life.
16. Have art and good music and theater and beauty.
17. Clean up fritters, those empty activities that tax your lifeforce and give you nothing, so that you'll have time for all of the above.

18. Take steps to break free from addiction in whatever form.
19. Find something you love within your work.
20. Get enough sleep.
21. Embark on new adventures.
22. Ask brave questions about what you really want.

If you can do these things, you will be burnout proof and you will have more zest for life.

As Sid told one interviewer, overall wellness has become the organizing umbrella for values clarification skills, plus eclectic tools from re-evaluation counseling, rational motive therapy, reality therapy, psychosynthesis, group dynamics, communication skills work, and more. All these modalities, he said, help people bridge the gap between what they say and do in the area of overall wellness.

He said, "Values realization has a unique contribution to make. It's a piece that other approaches often are missing. Values clarification and values realization move beyond the rhetoric of understanding, of insight, of a-ha. We have specific, prescribed tools which allow people to take their lives in their own hands, to take charge, and to move forward with a rational viable scheme that promotes clarity. Raths used to say that the outcome of values clarification would be that people would be more productive, their lives would be more purposeful, they would do clearer critical thinking, they would have a deeper set of human relationships, and above all –and I can still see the twinkle in his eye—he would say, 'They will have more zest in their lives because they have values clarification in their lives'."

Life and Death

To find fulfillment, a person needs three things: to be able to love, to be able to be loved, and to find a sense of purpose in your work and your life. But there comes a point in working through what you want your life to be that you must also consider death. People dread this subject and view it with great anxiety, yet, as Sid and his co-author Joel Goodman wrote in an article called "A Study of Death through the Celebration of Life," there is nothing so inevitable in our lives as dying.

The article lays out some strategies for exploring "the issue of death without it becoming a morbid and fearful experience." He adapted these exercises to help young students examine the issue of death in a "positive and meaningful way," and they are also very helpful for an adult to think through. Here's a sample:

The Coat of Arms

Outline a six-panel shield like a knight's coat of arms. In each section, draw a symbol for one of these things: what would your friends miss about you if you died; what you would give your life for; what's the closest you ever came to dying; who close to you has died; what are you doing to live a long, healthy life; and if you were told you had a year left to live, what would you do in that year. As the article says, "Too often in life we realize the value of someone or something only after it is gone. The coat of arms strategy is one way to help students appreciate themselves and others while they are still here."

In response to this exercise, I remembered a moment when I could have died. I wrote:

> *"I was eleven. I was swimming with a girlfriend in the ocean. We were holding onto a black inner tube. My brother was an excellent swimmer, and he said that I should swim by myself and not hold onto the tube. He wanted the tube. I didn't know how to swim, and my friend was trying to survive and pushing me under to save herself as I was trying to hold on to her. My brother's back was turned. But a lifeguard saw, and he pulled me and my friend out of the water."*

I was happier considering what I was doing to live a long, healthy life. My list in included everything from playing to taking vitamins, including prayer, laughter, long showers, a good support group, wearing a seat belt, having a loving relationship and trying to make smart choices.

Asking the Hard Question

Consider a few questions about death that evoke various value-based discussions, such as:

- Have you been to a funeral? How do you feel about it? Why do we have funerals?
- Do you believe in life after death? How does that affect how you live?
- Would you donate your body to science? Why or why not?
- If a person with a painful disease asks to die, should he or she be allowed to be put to death?

The Obituary

To illustrate our individual responsibility for the quality of our lives, try writing your obituary. Consider the values each statement represents as you discuss what you will be remembered for and what you contributed. If this seems difficult, begin by writing an obituary for a pet.

The Epitaph

What would you want engraved on your tombstone? Can you create an "accurate, nutshell summary" of your life and what mattered to you?

Keep in mind, Simon and Goodman conclude, "Values clarification exercises are designed to provide us with opportunities to identify and build on what we have in common, but also to help us more fully understand and respect the ways in which we are different and unique."

I think everyone is familiar with Elizabeth Kubler-Ross's psychological stages in preparation for death, though not everyone understands that these stages do not always unfold in order, and that each stage can recur. Everyone dies in their own way. Kubler-Ross outlined these stages: denial, anger, bargaining, depression—which is preparatory grief—and acceptance. This is not resignation, and it's not either happy or sad. Instead it is more positive. As one dying patient said, "I am going very peacefully from this garden into the next one."

The feelings of anger and depression are hard to express, especially with your grieving friends and family around you, but as a helper, you can give the person permission to express their feelings by saying something like, "I would be really upset and angry if this were to happen to me." When the person can express anger in a supportive setting, he or she may then reach a more emotionally content stage. However the person answers, accept it, whatever it is.

When I was a student at FIU, I learned so much from Erick Erikson writings on the eight stages in a person's life cycle. Erikson, a psychoanalyst, teacher, and artist, wrote about this progression of personal development in which social drives play as important a role as biological urges in a human being's maturation from childhood to old age. Each stage harbors a special crisis the person must work through in order to move to the next stage. He gave me tremendous insight. It was such an eye-opener. I kept reading it, seeing myself and my children evolving through these stages. I've read it over and over all these years. You can identify people and what level they have reached through these stages. You never know when a person is going to move on to another level.

He wrote, "The struggle between the negatives and positives in each crisis must be fought through successfully if the next developmental stage is to be reached. Yet, no victory is completely or forever one."

Erickson's eight stages are:

1. *Infancy: Trust vs. Mistrust*—The infant's main job is to develop the cornerstone of a healthy personality. The danger, most acute in the second half of the first year, is that discontinuities in care may increase a natural sense of loss, as the child gradually recognizes his separateness from his mother, and can result in a basic sense of mistrust that may last throughout his life.

2. *Early childhood: Autonomy vs. Shame and Doubt*—Children need to develop their sense of will and control, including through toilet training. If deprived, they could learn to feel ashamed.

3. *Play age: Initiative vs. Guilt*—Children have freer movement and can develop their imagination. They begin to communicate and to develop a conscience. If adults overburden this ability to feel guilty, children can develop an abiding sense of being bad.

4. *School age: Industry vs. Inferiority*—The child wants to learn how to do and make things with others, through which he gains the capacity to enjoy work. The danger in this period is the development of a sense of inadequacy in a child whose efforts earn no recognition.

5. *Adolescence: Identity vs. Identity diffusion*—With puberty and sexual maturity, young people must integrate their childhood identity with their biological and social growth. The developmental risk is "because of youth's tendency to total commitment," teens who don't live up to parental or societal expectations may decide to become exactly what their parents or community do not want.

6. *Young adult: Intimacy vs. Isolation*—Only as young people begin to feel more secure in their identity, are they able to establish intimacy with themselves (with their inner life) and with others, both in friendship and eventually in a love-based relationship. A person who cannot enter wholly into an intimate relationship because of the fear of losing his or her identity may develop a deep sense of isolation.

7. *Adulthood: Generativity vs. Self-absorption*—Erickson writes that generativity grows out of the intimacies of adulthood. A mature person cares about establishing and guiding the next generation. Without that concern, self-absorption and stagnation can develop.

8. *Senescence: Integrity vs. Disgust*—People who achieve a satisfying intimacy with others and who adapt to life's triumphs and disappointments as parents and co-workers reach the end of life with a certain ego-integrity and accept personal responsibility for what their life is and was and of its place in the flow of history.

This stage brings one inevitably to considering death, and that line of thinking also has its consequences, as Howard Koestenbaum enumerated:

1. "Man cannot escape death—real or symbolic.

2. "Once he has recognized and admitted the inevitability of his death, the individual is on the way to becoming courageous, fearless and decisive.

3. "By remembering the certainty and finality of death, man immediately sees the urgency of concentrating on the essentials.

4. "Only through the constant awareness of death will an individual achieve integrity and consistency with his principles.

5. "The man who knows he will die wastes no time in attacking the problems of finding meaning and fulfillment in life.

6. "The vitality of death lies in that it makes almost impossible the repression of unpleasant but important realities.

7. The realization of my death leads to strength.

8. To accept death means to take charge of one's life.

9. The thought of death urges one to assume a total plan of life.

10. The thought of death enables men to laugh off vicissitudes and pains.

To this, I would add Sid's teaching that the only reason to look at death is to reaffirm the celebration of life. In 1980, in one of his workshops, I was assigned to write my own obituary. This is what I came up with:

> *Sharing my journey for personal growth might help others in their effort of personal growth as well. It is a long process that does not stop until you die. That's why I am trying to fill my book with ways I learned to grow personally through my life. Perhaps it will inspire my family and friends.*

One of the special things about learning from Sid Simon and becoming an instructor is that I became friends with him and his wife, Suzanne. After my horrible car accident, he wrote to me, "I am so sad to hear about your car accident, but so damn glad you are alive and healing. We miss you. It's been too long. Send us some news to bring us up to date on your kids, etc. Are you still in love? (He was asking about Herman, my partner at the time of the accident.) How does it bloom? We are. It truly gets better and better each day…I send lots of love, lots of good memories, and lots of gratitude for all you did to advance the work for all of us. Heal well. Heal well."

Virginia Satir

My teacher Virginia Satir (1916–1988), was a pioneer in family therapy and a person of international significance in her field.

Virginia once sent me this note: "Esther, Thank you for all your help. I have learned from you. I wish you all the best." She also thanked me "for a job well done." Her kind words meant the world to me because of how much I learned from her.

Virginia's goal as a teacher was clear. As she said, "I want to empower people so that they can do their own work." She warned against the "tyranny of the one 'right' way," and urged exploration and in-depth investigation. "What I want," Virginia said, "is to make the hidden obvious, the abstract concrete, the implicit explicit, and the covert overt."

I drew from what Virginia called her "Self-Esteem Maintenance Kit" (*©1988, Avanta Network*). It had five components designed to keep you "in touch with your caring, loving, emotional and intellectual self" as you engage in a constant process of growing.

She urges us to keep this toolkit with us all the time to remind us of our own magnificence, and to assure us we can take what fits us and leave the rest behind. These tools are (quoting Virginia):

1. **The Golden Key**—This opens the door to the sanctuary within yourself so you can rejoice in the person you are. To open any door, use this in conjunction with the other components of this toolbox. If you face a closed door, use this key to open it.

2. **Detective Hat**—This gives you the ability to figure out life's puzzles with the clues you are given. This tool helped me learn to look and move ahead, but without judging.

3. **Wisdom Box**—This holds the knowledge of your unique inner resources. These treasures help you move into the awareness everyone is equipped with as a human being.

4. **Medallion**—With "yes" on one side and "no" on the other side, this enables you to accept what fits and discard what does not. However, you must be willing to say yes or no.

5. **Courage Stick**—This empowers you to ask for what you want and make your wishes come true. Virginia said she placed in our hands to "give you the power to move ahead."

Virginia formed her organization, Avanta, which means "to move forward," in 1977. Its philosophy is that "there is never enough time to learn about our humanness." All her teachings opened up that quest for her students who are learning her approach to family therapy. Her miracle is in teaching others how to become bridges for those in pain.

She made us aware of both our strength and our vulnerability. Virginia said that if our families teach us, "I will still love you, no matter what you say or do," we will feel safe. To open their energy, people need that sense of safety. However, they can achieve it other ways, including by recognizing that, "God's spirit is in all of us." She helps people see themselves through that spirit, so they can feel safe enough to open their energy.

My notes on Virginia's classes and books are very extensive, and these many years later, I can't say what is my synthesis of what I heard in class and what is a direct quote from Virginia. I will put her sayings in quotation marks when I'm sure, and I freely credit her with all this wisdom. She had an amazing sense of each person's depth and potential.

In her book *Peoplemaking,* Virginia taught that people's feeling of worth comes from their families of origin. She said, "I am convinced that there are no genes that carry the feeling of worth. It is learned" in the family. You learn to feel worthwhile at home, and your children are learning that from your family right now. Every word, facial expression, gesture or action from a parent gives children a message about their personal worth.

As an adult, however, you can build or rebuild yourself. You have the tools to survive and thrive, to become close to other people, to be productive and to make sense and order out of the world. In "A Goal of Living" (December 1970), Virginia wrote this short verse:

> *"I own me, therefore*
> *I can engineer me.*
> *I am me and I am okay."*

A person with high self-esteem is a source of integrity, honesty, responsibility and compassion. Those who know they matter bestow love in the knowledge that the world is better because they are here. Given appreciation of their own worth, they can appreciate the worth of others.

Those with low self-esteem also expect the worst of others and, sadly, that is often what they elicit. In self-defense, they hide behind distrust and live with apathy, loneliness and isolation. This leads to fear, and reinforces it. Those who live in fear find it hard to risk new ways of solving problems, to try closeness and to see, hear and think clearly.

In *Peoplemaking,* Virginia teaches readers how to manage fear, which, she says, relates to some future threat. As soon as you face that challenge, the fear will disappear. People need help to learn if they are managing themselves negatively with fear or positively. However, being fearful is something people can address.

There is nothing bad about being scared. Fearful people can find their inner resources and become more truly themselves.

One step is to start with resources you already have and to communicate about the factors that seem to threaten your health, intimacy and productivity. People need openness and awareness to live in freedom and to discard things that are holding them back. Sharing and trust increase your energy. Therapy puts people in touch with themselves. Virginia would say that people come for help when they can no longer endure being alone and they need help becoming aware, asking for what they want, and changing their context.

Virginia teaches other therapists that "everyone has everything they need and a good therapist can give it to them." You can help people as they go on their journey to become more able to see and hear themselves and others, and to make different kinds of connections.

However, while you can explain and help people, you can't get them to do something they refuse to do or aren't ready to do. People need a way of viewing their situation before they can act. Help them connect to their life force and nurture it.

Each person is a source of energy and light, but people often shut down their light out of fear of being vulnerable, even though we are all vulnerable. If you feel wounded and need to know that you will be okay, analyze what has wounded you. There are three kinds of wounds:

1. Physical—Some part of your body is injured.
2. Intellectual—You don't know what you're doing and even feel that you hate yourself.
3. Emotional—You may inflict this wound on yourself by telling yourself that you're no good, that you're not a worthwhile person.

Healing these wounds begins with realizing that you have to nurture yourself (something you must do before you can nurture others). Understanding that you are worthy and can help others feel worthy starts with listening and working on new possibilities. But, as Virginia taught, you must allow yourself to heal; if you continue to focus on your wounds, you will keep the symptoms.

For example, if you still worry about the negative messages you heard from your family, make a tape listing all those negative parts. (I took this to mean all the negative things that my mother told me about myself.) Making a list is a creative way to identify these negatives and rid yourself of them. Then make a list of all the positive parts of yourself, to build your appreciation and self-realization. My new list taught me the essence of who I am and all that I was capable of becoming. It gave me hope, which all wounded people need.

Try to reframe negatives into positives. Virginia helped me understand that my parents did the best they could. If they had known better, they would have done better. Children can't take care of their parents' bad feelings. They are only human, like their parents. Children also can't carry the burdens of their parents, whether that is trauma or alcoholism or drugs and the like.

Wounded people may have wounded relationships that they need to rebuild into healing relationships. You can do effective things to address these wounds, including listening, learning, and sharing. You can work on what you are able to do and collect new possibilities. Some people address their wounds in ways that, ultimately are not effective, such as taking drugs and drinking. People cannot change the events that happen to them, but they can cope with these events. Life is about solving problems and finding ways to cope.

As Virginia said, "The problem is not the problem; the problem is coping with the problem."

To cope, I had to learn to see my sub-personalities, the negative sides of myself that exist because I allow them to exist within me. These will always be part of me, but if I "resist them, they will persist," Virginia taught. Instead, I have to stop playing out those negative parts of myself, and learn to appreciate myself instead. Then, the negative parts of myself won't be me. Instead, my positive facets will be the conductor of my life. That knowledge enabled me to heal and to help other people heal. Helping other people and having a positive impact on their lives has been my main goal. That is one reason I have dedicated myself to lifelong learning and growing.

There is another part of this lesson I learned from Virginia when my children were young adults: if I can see the positive parts of myself and appreciate all that I am, I will see that in my children, too. And, even more, they will reflect the positive sides of themselves. You must have a positive identification with your parents to have a positive identification with yourself. That identification must be based on their essence, not necessarily their behavior.

However, you have to take the risk to learn to appreciate yourself, forgive yourself, celebrate yourself and love yourself and your unique presence. I gave myself permission to love myself, and that helped me become strong. I learned that we all have resources in our treasure box and we can choose what we pull out and use. Ask yourself, "What do you want to do." Defeat what you do not want to do.

Your family teaches you how to behave in the world and give you your sense of trust. A child gets validation from its parents. However, as Virginia established in her work, some people experiencing a painful childhood basically stop growing at age five. The pain of recognition or blame becomes too much. When she works with people who were traumatized as children, she first goes through what they have seen and been through, how they interpret it and how they feel now. Then she gives them the gift of equality, the idea that we are all equal—that no one is better than you.

Healing begins with that clarity. Every family has some dysfunction, so everyone comes from that basis. All of us are "wounded healers" in some way.

Virginia also teaches new parents how to nurture themselves so they can nurture others. Almost everyone has to learn how to nurture. These lessons made me realize that my mother never told me what I did to upset her, perhaps because she could not. She never verbalized what made her angry with me. But often, as Virginia says, people in our lives are often unaware that they have wounded us. I had to learn that it is okay to love myself and to feel good about myself.

She shows that instead of being a boss, a parent can become a guide, based on how they share with their children. They can give the gift of connection, even using humor, which helps people connect. If a child is doing something wrong, take him or her into your arms, draw them close with love and build their self-esteem. Create a connect that leaves the child room to grow. Have confidence and faith in the process of growing.

Everyone you meet starts out as a stranger, but Virginia teaches us how to bridge that gap by considering how you see someone new. Realize that each individual is unique and original. No two people are alike. When you meet someone new, have a sense of celebration. When you get in touch with your uniqueness, you can recognize and celebrate it in others. Then become consciously aware of your presence—and the other person's. Make yourself fully present.

When a parent—or a person in a conversation—is preoccupied, they aren't dealing with the child or the other person. You need to give yourself conscious permission to be really present, to relax, be loose, think "I love me," and value yourself and what you are bringing to the encounter and the relationship.

In these circumstances, your physical persona matters. Work on making eye contact at the other person's level. If you are meeting an adult, shake hands from no more than a half-a-yard away. You gain an awareness of the other person from touching, a sense of their physical self. This is something we've mostly lost during the Covid pandemic, but I hope we will get it back in time. No one in the world can do everything alone.

Therapists should realize, "The world is a better place because of me being centered in healing." The modeling and presence of the therapist helps people who are emotionally starving and need to be healed. To heal them, they have to become centered as well. They need to get their parts together. Virginia worked to help people stand on their own feet. This is especially important for people who have been wounded and feel like victims. They may have a low sense of self and lack the courage to take a step.

The therapist must make contact with each person by being very aware of who the person is. Be aware of their struggle and what steps they need to take so they can connect, relax and become centered. The more energy people have to use to defend themselves, the less energy they have to be creative, to say "I'm willing to take a risk even if I feel I may make a mistake because I will be learning."

The therapist can empower people to be themselves, to feel worthwhile, to recognize that the only way out of their fear is through that fear. People who fear losing a loved one or facing some other loss must realize that life is always changing and will always change. In fact, the only thing you can count on is change. Any good or bad relationship has some element of going into the unknown.

People who are wounded may need to go through a healing process of learning to be more real, finding their real selves. Recovery has six stages: survival, during which you learn how you got wounded and got awakened to being wounded, followed by awakening, dealing with core issues, transformation, integration and spirituality. Working through core issues alone can take three or five years of therapy, perhaps working individually and in a group and writing a journal as you learn to be safe and heed your own needs.

Each person has different core issues, such as learning to love, to handle conflict, to shed a false self, to care for yourself (as opposed to being egoistic or narcissistic), to interact, to commit, to dealing with difficult character traits or difficult people. To recover, people must name their issues so they can focus on them. As you bring your core issues into consciousness, Virginia taught, then you can move toward self-actualization through recovery, integration and wholeness.

Every adult faces the three ways individuals learn from their family.

1. How I treat myself.

2. How I treat others.

3. How others treat me.

As you come to regard your family as your school of learning, Virginia warns that some of what you will learn through reflection could be hurtful. These lessons include the message that you were supposed to be perfect and couldn't be, because no one can. They may include the idea that you are never allowed to get angry at people you love, though everyone gets angry.

Virginia explained anger as "a brave attempt on the part of a person to survive—it is like a fire extinguisher in an emergency." She explained, "Disappointment doesn't show when it is covered in anger."

You may find yourself caught between the concept that you can never leave your family and that you must flee from them. Each person must identify his or her core issues and work through them. The solution is to live in the present, in the now, based on your internal direction, your heart, and your ability to go beyond the injuries you've received in life. Once you see that you can have agency, that you can do differently, you will realize that your thoughts are meaningful and important. You can extract from life the elements that fit you, now, and leave the rest. We can be choosers.

This requires seeing your feelings as your helpers and your energy, but not letting them control you. Give yourself permission to use your energy to make choices even about your internal dialogue. You always have a choice to change, but you want to keep your mind open about decision making in confidence that you can drive your own ship.

Realize that achieving mental health has a spiritual component. You want to be aware of a higher power and heed these changes:

Stop judging = start exploring

Having to be right = wanting to be real

Giving up being anxious about life in exchange =
being excited about life

Stop having limits = So you can have infinite possibilities.

You can leave a limiting context to achieve movement, flexibility, reality and peace. Our hearts know what is positive. We have to open up to see the whole picture and to look beyond the threat of the negative. Love carries a more complete picture.

As Virginia, who was also an accomplished poet, once wrote:

"In order to really live
I had to start letting go
Like waves in the ocean."

Consider what elements in your belief system make you feel good and whole. Seek your core self through discovery, growth, celebration, connection and, perhaps metaphorically, returning home. Some things that used to make you feel good—like money and power—may not be what make you feel good now or what feeds your spiritual side. Virginia teaches that you must treat yourself as valuable first and leave self-hatred behind before you can treat others with value.

This is a process of becoming more fully human and giving your mind a message of appreciation. We all have the possibility to change, to become more aware of ourselves, to learn from crisis. What we do follows how we are feeling inside, so seeing God inside of you is a gift your give yourself.

Develop a new picture of yourself. As Virginia always asks, what would you like to have happen that is not happening now? Work toward the fantasy you want to fulfill. Develop your picture of yourself. Ask, "what have you done with your dreams?" Give yourself permission to ask for what you want. Determine what you need for yourself.

Quotes from Virginia Satir

"I have the tools to survive. What I need is to learn how to be close to others without fear, and to make sense and order out of the world of people and things outside me and things inside me, until I can own myself. I cannot engineer me, but with courage and help, I can become me. I will be okay."

"No matter how much alike we are, we are still different. No matter how different we are, we are still alike."

"When I take care of me, I give something to you."

"The most important thing is when the stars come on in people's eyes."

"You never outgrow your need for growth."

"The wish to do something is not the same as taking action."

"Behind every question is a 'do you love me?' message."

"We pay heavily for the assumption that our view is the only one."

"The essence of the change process is the effective use of self."

"There is a difference between what I feel and how I act on that feeling."

"Growth is a commitment to go into unknown territory."

"Tears are not the hurt; tears are the healing."

"Only a baby is not afraid to love. To truly love, you have to tremble."

"Learn how to use your hands for helping. Things your mouth can't do, your hands can do!"

"I am in the world to help people grow."

Virginia Satir's lessons and poems endure in her writings. Her books include:

- *Peoplemaking* (1972)
- *Conjoint Family Therapy* (1983)
- *Satir Step by Step: A Guide to Creating Change in Families* (1984)
- *The New Peoplemaking* (1988)

And published posthumously:

- *Meditations and Inspiration* (1995)
- *Self-Esteem* (1995)
- *The Satir Model: Family Therapy and Beyond* (2006)
- *Your Many Faces: The First Step to Being Loved* (2009)
- *Making Contact* (2020), from The Virginia Satir Global Network

Other experts have written several books about her and her teachings, including:

- *In Her Own Words: Virginia Satir: Selected Papers: 1963–1983* by John Banmen (2008)
- *Systematic Training in the Skills of Virginia Satir* (Marital, Couple & Family Counselling) by Sharon Loeschen (1997)
- *Virginia Satir: Foundational Ideas* by Barbara Jo Brothers (2016)
- *Well-Being Writ Large: The Essential Work of Virginia Satir,* Brothers (2019)
- *Virginia Satir: The Patterns of Her Magic,* Steve Andreas (2020)
- *Simple but Profound Sayings of Virginia Satir,* Banmen and Loeschen (2020)

I read the book* How Good Do We Have to Be *by Rabbi Harold Kushner. I learned a lot from these excellent reviews and want to share them.

According to an article in *Parade Magazine,* September 8, 1996, page 9, a dying congregant told the Rabbi that she finally learned you don't have to be perfect to be worth loving. I only wish I had known that sooner. I thought I had to be perfect! We need to give ourselves permission to be human, to try and to stumble. Life is not a spelling bee where one mistake wipes out all we've done right.

"Why does God make human life so complicated?" Maybe it is because God loves goodness more than perfection and apprcciates our struggle to achieve good as morally preferable to our being programmed to be perfect. If God could not love flawed, imperfect people, God would be very lonely, because imperfect people are the only ones around. If we can't accept and love people with all their imperfections, we condemn ourselves to loneliness, as well.

We need to stop blaming our parents for making mistakes in raising us. Our children need to know that we will not stop loving them anytime they do wrong. Without that assurance, Rabbi Kushner says, we don't teach our children to be perfect. We teach them to be liars.

The Rabbi goes on to say that the essence of married life is not romance but forgiveness. Romantic love needs to deny and overlook flaws. But mature love sees the faults in ourselves and in the ones we love and is capable of loving flawed people.

We need to give ourselves permission to be human, to try and stumble, to be momentarily weak and to feel shame, but to overcome that shame with moments of strength, courage and generosity. We need to learn to define ourselves not by our worst moments, but by our typical ones.

I love his analogy: "Life is like the baseball season, where even the best team loses at least a third of its games and even the worst team has its days of being brilliant. The goal is not to win every game but to win more than you lose. And, if you do that often enough, in the end you may find you have won it all!

In an article in the *Dade Jewish Journal,* written by staff writer Debra Wallace during the week of November 14 to 20, 1996, Rabbi Kushner emphasized that we do not need to be perfect to be loved. "If we are afraid to make a mistake because we have to maintain the pretense of perfection," he said, "we will never be brave enough to try anything new or anything challenging. We will only do things that are guaranteed to turn out right. We will never learn. We will never grow."

Rabbi Kushner says his books are based on his perception of religion as primarily a form of healing and cleansing, as opposed to judging and condemning. The great lesson from his book is about forgiving people who have hurt you. That is what people respond to, even more so than forgiving themselves. We must learn to forgive ourselves for our mistakes.

Rabbi Kushner says you don't have to define yourself by the moment when you need forgiveness; instead, define yourself by what you do best.

Despite all the conditional love and rejection one receives in life, Rabbi Kushner says that one person can be the key. What I have found, the rabbi says, "is if you have one person who gives you the message that he or she loves you as you are, it will be enough to carry you through." For me, that was my aunt Sophie, to whom I dedicate this book.

In an article in "Family Circle," November 21, 1995, the Rabbi says, "Everything that God has created is potentially holy. Our task as humans is to find that holiness in seemingly unholy situations. When we can do this, we will have learned to nurture ourselves. But can we find the holiness in the struggle for life?

He defines the Jewish religion as the science of taking the ordinary and making it holy. The idea is to try to find the holiness in everything. Food. Sex. Earning and spending money. Having children. Everything can be seen as a miracle and as part of God's plan. When we can truly see this, we nourish our souls.

Nourishing our souls can be compared to nourishing our body. The same thing is true of spiritual nourishment. When we perform acts of kindness—when we give to charity or forgive someone who may have hurt us—we get a wonderful feeling inside.

Rabbi Kushner says that each of us was put on this Earth to fulfill his or her potential for humanity. The soul is the part of us that makes us truly human. The soul is not a physical entity. It refers to everything about us that it is not physical—our values, memories, identity, sense of humor. Since the soul represents the parts of the human being that are not physical, it cannot get sick and it cannot die. Your soul cannot disappear.

The soul craves two distinct types of nourishment: public and private.

Rabbi Kushner says he is a very public person. He feels that he nourishes his soul through contacts with others. He needs contact with and feedback from other people. For me, I love to feel I am part of a team. Some people nurture their soul in a more private way, through meditation, study and self-improvement.

When we are confronted with a problem we fear, we shouldn't ask God to take away the problem. Instead, we should pray that he gives us the strength to deal with the problem. Religion cannot change facts; it can change the way we relate to them.

The Rabbi explains that the religious thinker Martin Buber defined the difference between theology and religion by saying that theology is "talking about God" and religion is "experiencing God."

We experience God when we pray, when we are helpful and kind, and when we overcome bad habits, addictions and pettiness in our lives. Ultimately, I believe that spiritual growth is like climbing a ladder. We climb slowly step-by-step. We solidify our footing on each step, then we move onto the next step. Each step nourishes our soul.

Harry Sloan

I studied extensively with Harry Sloan, a masterful teacher of using psychosynthesis as a comprehensive way to understand human psychology, involving the spirit as well as the mind and body. He taught about imagination as well as rationality, and saw the will as pivotal in human development. I have broken down some of the lessons I learned from Harry into explaining psychosynthesis, the concept of subpersonalities,

What Is Psychosynthesis?

Psychosynthesis, I wrote in notes I took many years ago, is an approach to human growth that expresses the will of the higher self through love and wisdom, the higher self's two fundamental qualities. This inclusive strategy for understanding growth stems from the early work of Venetian psychiatrist Roberto Assagioli dating back to 1911, and based partly on the esoteric teachings of Alice Bailey. A colleague of Sigmund Freud, Assagioli held that Freud did not pay enough attention to the higher aspects of human beings, and so he pursued a broader idea. As a student of the world's philosophies and spiritual traditions, Assagioli brought a psychospiritual dimension to psychology, as he presented in his 1965 book, *Psychosynthesis: A Manual of Principles and Techniques.*

People have a natural drive to develop themselves, to grow and achieve their highest worth. Psychosynthesis facilitates that natural drive. In its broadest sense, psychosynthesis is a point of view, an attitude, that infuses human actions with wisdom and love. It works with psychology, education, medicine, religion, the social sciences, philosophy and other disciplines that address each individual's consciousness.

The heart of psychosynthesis is understanding how to reach the essence within oneself and other people to develop each person's inherent wisdom and intuition. As Harry taught his students, psychosynthesis is a creative therapy for understanding the process of reaching for and building this essence in yourself and others.

Within that context, he taught us how to use the tools and methods of psychosynthesis to help people achieve a balance—a synthesis—among the various facets of themselves and to release and transform their blocked energies to lovingly translate psychological awareness and insight into deliberate behavioral change.

Drawing from an article I've saved for so long that its origin is now illegible, I want to add a few background points to consider: Traditional psychoanalysis recognized both a lower consciousness, the source of biological drives, and a higher superconscious, the realm of our more highly evolved impulses, like altruistic love and will, humanitarian action, artistic and scientific inspiration, and philosophic and spiritual insight. People suffer not only when their base drivers are suppressed, but also when they fail to recognize and accept their highest nature.

The superconscious is available to each of us, in varying degrees, and can provide energy, inspiration, and direction. Psychosynthesis offers ways to build a bridge to the superconscious, the part of our inner selves where we can find real wisdom. Its techniques include guided imagery, self-identification, mediation, development of the will, symbolic art work, journal keeping, idea models and other approaches. However, its emphasis is not on methods, but on fostering ongoing growth.

An article from the newsletter of the German branch of the Association for Humanistic Psychology explains, "Personal psychosynthesis concentrates on building a personality which is efficient and relatively free from emotional blocks and which can satisfy its own needs, direct its energy constructively, use failure creatively, and command its psychological functions. Transpersonal psychosynthesis explores regions beyond ordinary awareness, areas of mystery and wonder called the superconscious."

I also want to draw briefly, for background, from Dr. Graham C. Taylor's presentation "The Essentials of Psychosynthesis," presented in Montreal in 1967. He ran through the basic concepts of psychosynthesis that I learned later from Harry Sloan. Taylor, a visionary, warned even then that the vast changes in our technological and social environment will lead to profound personal changes, and that psychology itself will have to evolve accordingly.

The processes of psychotherapy and personal growth involve a person discovering and contacting his or her true self. To this purpose, psychosynthesis incorporates Jung's four psychic functions—sensation, feeling, thought and intuition—and adds three others, imagination, will and human drives. Psychosynthesis is concerned with developing the will in four stages: uncovering unconscious motives and their rationales; decision making based on reality and expressed positively; affirmation or confirmation of decisions once made; and planning and organizing our ongoing activities in a clearly outlined program.

In that way, psychosynthesis is active. With the guidance of a therapist, patients work to contact and discover their inner selves—often continuing growth that was interrupted as they led their lives. The therapist helps the patient unite opposing attitudes and tendencies to resolve internal conflicts, defensiveness and resistance and to achieve self-realization.

Whatever your attitude is, your behavior will show it. Once you become clear about your attitude, you can decide where you want to hang out. Your attitude is everything, positive or negative. A piece of research called the Pygmalion Study found that if someone working in a lab with rats thinks his or her rat is smart or slow, over time, that is how your rat behaves. Your attitude is everything.

Identifying your true attitude feeds into the first of the four steps of attaining self-realization: coming to know your personality thoroughly, controlling its various elements, realizing your true self, and forming or reforming your personality around this new center. To achieve the last step, people formulate a plan of action, perhaps aiming for an ideal image or pushing through known obstacles to deepen their internal congruency and communication. This calls for bringing the right energies to the fore, developing neglected areas of the personality, and coordinating various psychological energies to create a firm organization of the personality.

Professionals can use psychosynthesis to treat psychiatric disturbances or to help "normal" people grow in self-realization. The key concept of psychosynthesis is developing the unified, integrated self as a center of awareness and will.

Subpersonalities

Roberto Assagioli spoke of the existence in each person of differing—and sometimes conflicting—subpersonalities. In a 1986 article, "Opening to the Inner Light," Ralph Metzner of Jeremy P. Tarcher, Inc., wrote that in Assagioli's view, people unconsciously identify with these personalities and, in time, become aware of "them as roles we unconsciously play out. Some have suggested the metaphor of the self as a kind of orchestra, with many different parts playing together. The task of transformation, then, is to attune and harmonize the different musicians and instruments of the personality.

I've saved a book chapter, "Subpersonalities and the possibility of synthesis," that sheds further light on people as dynamic, contradictory beings who experience both trouble and joy as life changes, from childhood to adolescence (stages where personality development may be more visible) to adulthood. As life changes and brings new challenges, the book notes, "we often feel at the mercy of forces we only dimly perceive and are often swayed by passions we did not know we possessed."

The concept of subpersonalities, the idea that "in each of us is a crowd," says that each person contains many selves. In the view of psychosynthesis, the interaction of those personal, innate qualities with our families and our environment creates our personality traits.

Experts from William James in the early 1900s to Carol Dweck (*Mindset: The New Psychology of Success*) today have discussed the differences between healthy and sick ways of living, between open and fixed mind-sets, and how they affect personal growth. James believed that some people have a unity that emanates from a naturally happy, spiritual center and strives for growth, while other selves are divided and vulnerable. Working with subpersonalities often means considering unconscious forces that haunt people, often harking back to childhood, such as trauma or hardship with their parents. People carry repressed traits that can emerge in times of illness or trouble. In fact, psychosynthesis assumes that each characteristic, somewhere, has its opposite, and that everyone carries aspects of this dichotomy.

Consider the instruments of that inner orchestra: some may be out of tune, some may play chaotically, some may not be ready to play at all. The conductor, the I, must choose the right score, bring in more instruments as needed, heed the neglected players, and "as we get to know what we have," my long-saved chapter explains, "we may decide to change the tune and play a different kind of music, constantly modifying it throughout our lives...This question of knowing what we do, knowing the implications and significance of what we do and are, is, Assagioli and Jung believed, part of the human task."

Thus, some subpersonalities are forces for growth, and some push against change. Some cling to order and identity, some embrace growth. This tension occurs in every system, individual and society, the pull of safety and the push of change. Subpersonalities also manifest on a continuum of love—the quest for acceptance and warm relationships—and will, manifesting as the power to control the environment versus the urge to modify it. psychosynthesis teaches that we need both love and will. Assagioli outlined seven qualities of will—energy, mastery, concentration, determination, persistence, initiative, and organization—and he incorporated understanding and empathy into his view of love.

Psychosynthesis works with a person's subpersonalities to recognize, accept, coordinate, integrate and synthesize each one so it can contribute to the whole. Subpersonalities have negative and positive aspects, often contradictory, but a person must accept both aspects in order to integrate them.

"This does not make for homogeneity, however. It is possible to hold many contradictory elements in one's own personality…and be prepared to live with them with some understanding." Thus a Socialist can love art and a Christian can enjoy detective novels. "The concept of subpersonalities makes it more possible for one to accept the inconsistency within oneself with tolerance—and maybe that is a lesson that applies to the variety in the external world. It is multiplicity within unity which is the aim, not standardization.

"The aim of synthesis is a person basically in harmony with herself or himself, able to live with her own multiplicity and the variety of the world…from the still place, and able to contribute from that same place to others and the greater integration of the world. The aim of psychosynthesis is ambitious and on many levels."

Every personality has a flip side. Consider this list:

- The clinging vine / tenderness and gentleness
- The doormat / aggression
- The guru / holiness, righteousness
- The power player / leadership, administration, guidance
- The guilty party / responsibility for everyone's feelings
- The judge / clear-eyed
- The haggler / organized, gets things done, doesn't get cheated
- The fearful of rejection / love and intimacy
- The blamer / discerning

Every subpersonality has a basic need it tries to fulfill. That's its job. Each subpersonality seeks to protect its person, but wrongfully believes that it alone can do so. Many of its actions are based on this incorrect belief. The more a subpersonality is threatened, the stronger its beliefs become, though they will usually listen and yield to confrontation that lead to acceptance. Each subpersonality has its own energy limited to qualities it accepts. People generally have a dominant subpersonality. If it is strong enough, a person feels little internal conflict, but may be expressing only a narrow segment of his or her full potential.

You—or you and your therapist—can work with your subpersonalities to achieve internal unity.

First, ask what faces you present to the world. Become aware of your subpersonalities as you consider how you interact with different people and situations. List as many of your subpersonalities as you can.

Ask each one a few questions (not that you must or even can answer each query for each subpersonality). First, what is its name? Consider funny labels, like Bitchy Bertha, Top Dog, Know It All, Wimp or Clinging Vine. A little humor will help you detach from the subpersonality and direct it consciously.

Sketch its personality, its looks, its beliefs. What does it feel or want. Can you make a drawing of its essential qualities? Try to identify each subpersonality's strengths and weaknesses, its two (or more) facets. Then consider each one's prominence or centrality in your life, and how it interacts with your other subpersonalities.

Then consider what role you, as the "Self," has in mediating the subpersonalities' internal conflicts. As an objective, compassionate observer, what can you give it, how can you incorporate it or shape it?

The techniques for communicating with your subpersonalities can include writing a letter from the Self to the subpersonality, speaking aloud or silently to it, role-playing its two sides. Your role as the Self is to attempt to become centered and aligned.

In Harry Sloan's workshops, he would have us identify each character, asking "who am I?" Then we would try to express the conflict or tension, and discover the subpersonality's old habits or needs. That lead to exploring ways to respond and change, for instance, replacing an old need with a new one, so that we could reach resolution.

Throughout, one of Harry's key principles, was that you must be nonjudgmental in this process. Accept the negatives in yourself and look for the pearls.

He explained that subpersonalities often form in childhood. They serve a purpose, such as saving you from a difficult situation when you were little or fulfilling a basic physical, social or self-expressive need. To identify the need, identify the subpersonality. Ask what it is moving away from or toward. Trace its history. Ask how it has changed over time. This often involves going back to childhood and consider whether you were wounded or joyful, or sometimes both.

Before I use myself as a "case history" of how some of these dialogues work, I should also note that sometimes a subpersonality can be expressed as living in a part of your body. Your body parts can serve as windows or doors to get into the house of your personality and to consider your various facets.

When I first began to work with this idea, I drew a picture of my torso showing a gain of 20 pounds in two years of stress, but as I thought more about what was really bothering me, I changed to a drawing of my heart.

The sub-personality asking for attention was my negative self-image, an image I was creating by gaining weight. By focusing on my heart, instead, I turned to my connection with my inner self, my higher self. As I thought about who I really am—or was at the time—I realized I couldn't get to my heart, to the higher part of myself, as long as I dwelled on a negative self-image that kept telling me how fat I was.

To move ahead, I had to embrace having a big heart, seeing myself as a giver. I had to find the opposite to negativity by being positive. Instead of giving myself too much food, I had to realize that nourishment comes from above, from God, faith and trust. The message was, "Eat well and you will grow"—not physically, but spiritually. My negative self-image—that subpersonality—had me stuck in scolding myself, in looking down instead of reaching up.

Applying Harry Sloan's teaching became very clear to me at that point. I had to listen to myself with my ears, see with my eyes, and get out of my mouth so that a better self-image could emerge. If I could hear and see my higher self, I didn't have to be stuck in my negative subpersonality. I could become who I really am.

As I found in this instance, the more we get to know our subpersonalities, the more integrated and connected we become. If we are not aware of them, our subpersonalities can keep us stuck. I was finally able to make the connection from my heart to my higher self.

We do not get rid of our subpersonalities, so we have to get to know them and cherish them. Then we can see negative manifestations and replace them with their positive opposites, and we could put them in their place. As the conductor of your own inner orchestra, you can't let the tuba play during the flute solo.

When you see a subpersonality's negative traits emerging, think to yourself, "Here comes that rascal. I can't let it take over." Consider the power—and the positive flip side—of these sample subpersonalities:

- **Fearful Freddy**—If you never try, you'll never fail, but you'll be stuck in place.
- **Tight-lipped Terry**—What you don't reveal won't be used against you.
- **Little lawyer**—If you're right, you can win the argument, even if winning the argument meant losing the relationship. When I saw the little lawyer cropping up, I had to use more flute—gentle communication—and less bombastic tuba.
- **Never-enough Edna**—If you eat and keep eating, you don't have to feel.

- **Doormat Dora**—Maybe that person who is being mean will be nicer if I just agree with everything.
- **Poor me**—If you seem sad, they won't make it worse.
- **Do It Alone Don**—Do everything yourself. If you let other people do it, they'll just mess up and you'll be blamed.
- **Mean Mabel (or Max)**—If you show any weakness, people will be mean to you.
- **Dumpy Dora**—If you're frumpy, you won't have to compete. Of course, you're setting yourself up to lose.

I realized that I would see myself becoming my sub-personalities when I became needy and scared, sad and negative. I could pull them together when my attitude changed and I was positive and grateful. Then I could see myself leading the band, but I had to go inward to do it.

You have to connect with your essence to go deeper inward. You may not be able to solve things at your current level, but you can reach for more depth. When I felt safe, I could connect with my essence, and I could repeat these affirmations: Faith, Trust, Acceptance, Power and Love. I had to have faith in positive outcomes. I had to be open to myself and God to build trust.

With Faith, I understood that my results were not my own. I had to believe in positive outcomes. Acceptance required seeing others as they are, not as I want them to be. Power was already at hand, I just had to see that I had my own power. I didn't need a protector. I was not a victim. And the biggest lesson about love was that I had to allow another person to be able to love their way. Things didn't always have to be done my way.

One exercise you can do to focus on paying attention to your best facets is to write an advertisement about yourself and all that you have to share or give. Write in the mind-set of where you are going, even if you're not there yet. Consider what you would like to give and receive. For this exercise, after my divorce, I wrote:

> *A good-looking woman looking for a mature man who knows how to please a woman. I know how to please a man. I am a sensitive, caring and committed woman looking for a juicy relationship.*

Now, I never sent that, but I thought it was a pretty brave thing to write, and I did have to take a good look at how much I had to offer.

In October of 1983, I wrote this piece about another subpersonality, and I offer it to you as one way to think through the impact of some particular facet of yourself.

"My subpersonality was the little scared girl who was told never to fight, who believed she was pretty, sweet, kind and considerate. She had to be feminine. She believed that when she fell in love, her partner would protect her and would fight everything for her. She thought that it's the male who must fight and who is wise. As a child, I did not think I could survive on my own because I was so needy.

"I had to see the little scared girl and become aware of her as some part of me. I know she exists, but she is only one part of me. I am more than that part. I have other qualities. I am strong and connected when I become both the male and female parts, because I think the male figures in, and brings strength. Once I become whole, I must not give that away by idealizing someone else. I am the female and the male.

"I will integrate this awareness and not seek these qualities—like male wisdom—outside of myself from someone else. No one can do this for me. It's too much of a burden to put on another person in a relationship. That part of me that expects someone else (my children?) to fight for me when I need help. I am asking too much, especially if the fight is against their father."

I think the little, scared girl is why I stayed in my marriage for so long. I didn't fight with my husband. But as I got stronger, and grew, I became my own protector. I didn't need him to protect me anymore.

When I am not that little girl, that is, when I own myself, I can learn not to idealize a man—and then I won't be so easy to hurt. In the future, I won't expect a man to become what I need, and when he doesn't, I won't feel hurt.

I realized that I must not give away my power by making a man into my protector, into something I need, someone stronger than me, instead of owning my security myself. I realized that I should not become dependent and I should keep myself whole.

This study of subpersonalities is a way of seeing human nature through the multiplicity of small I's that make up a whole person. They aren't just a way of identifying part of yourself, but provide a way to integrate your many facets. Identifying your subpersonalities is a way of owning your own experiences, emotional mind-sets and reactions before you can synthesize them, which is the overall goal.

One psychosynthesis technique Harry used is called, "The Evening Review," which I will explain by drawing on a paper published years ago by the Psychosynthesis Institute in Palo Alto, California. "The Evening Review" calls on you to review your day in your mind just before falling asleep. Play the day back like a movie, beginning when you woke up. Look at your day as a detached observer, registering each phase without excitement. The aim is a "calm registering in consciousness of the meaning and patterns of the day, rather than a reliving of it." Consider making notes so you can become aware of patterns and trends.

One modification of "The Evening Review" calls on you to review your day from the point of view of your subpersonalities. The paper defines subpersonalities as, "The many diverse personages or psychological formations with our personality which have their own semi-independent activities, needs, and aims. Many of them are quite individual. Others are fairly common such as the Child, the Parent, the Seeker, the Clinger, the Poet or the Lonely One." Before you try to express the point of view of a subpersonality, pause to identify two or three active ones clearly in your mind.

This exercise is designed to help you get to know your subpersonalities, so keep it simple. The Institute suggests spending no more than 15 minutes a day considering these points:

- Which subpersonalities were dominant during the day, and what circumstances drew them out or shut them down. Did they conflict with one another?
- What were the qualities and limitations of each subpersonality? Did they help or hinder you?
- What did each one want? How would it shape your life if a subpersonality could have its own way completely?
- Were your subpersonalities in harmony with what you want to do, or were you catering to them? How did you harmonize or direct them?

Control Theory

The core of control theory is realizing that the only person you can control is yourself. The only human being whose behavior you control is you. And the only thing you can change is the way you act and think.

Each person sets out to define and fulfill his or her basic needs through the mechanism of how he or she thinks and behaves. From birth to death, you interact with other people, using your behavior to seek satisfaction of your needs. Even an infant has the capacity to know if it feels good or bad and to cry. It can't do much else, so it cries out if in need.

Those feelings—based on knowing whether our needs are being met or not—govern our behavior even as adults. When your basic needs are met, you feel good. When they are not, you feel bad. We start learning this at birth. These basic needs, beyond the necessities of survival, are: Belonging, power, freedom, fun, and then whichever of your needs isn't being met—and that's a different list for each person.

The purpose of life is to build your Real World, your Quality World. As you live your life, you're always making choices and decisions, and those acts and thoughts define what you allow to enter your Quality World.

Harry Sloan's Workshop

In October 1982, I had a four-day psychosynthesis workshop in my home for mental health professionals to study with Harry Sloan. I remember it well. Harry stayed in our home for four nights. My friend Gwen Succops helped me set up all the arrangements and became my closest friend for more than 50 years.

We learned in Harry's workshop that people have three basic needs: you must be able to love, be able to accept love, and you must have satisfaction in your work, or whatever your daily occupation may be. Giving love comes first, but I was all too familiar with what happens when someone can't accept love, because that describes my husband Alan. It was hard for him to be open to the feeling of being loved, understood and accepted.

Harry taught that learning at a certain level requires stretching and risking. I had to acknowledge that I had reached a stage in my life when I had to say what I meant instead of "the right thing" to say. I had to stop being concerned with pleasing everyone else. I had to learn that expressing your true feelings gives you agency and power, but all of that was risky.

I realized through working with Harry that I needed to give my love to my children, but that I didn't need to be angry with them for not making me feel loved. When I expected that, they would pull away. I had to believe that I am lovable without them telling me so.

I learned that I am strong and that I could build up my own strength by making up my mind about how to see my actions and theirs. I gave away my power for 27 years. I learned that, instead, I could claim it, to be independent and meet my own needs.

Harry emphasized such personal process work. He taught us to affirm the qualities in ourselves that we saw in other people. Determine what quality can help you grow and get what you need. Instead of feeling anxious and rejected when someone doesn't see the good I'm offering, I had to see it in myself, to focus on the qualities I appreciated in myself: openness, courage, acceptance and caring. If you need to reach for such self-acceptance, think back to a time in your life when you experienced the quality of appreciation or caring or openness, and embrace it.

I had to connect with those qualities in myself, to say to other people, "I would like you to see my openness, my courage, my strength and love, my fear of being hurt, my caring. I would like you to see me." Personal process work gave me a deeper sense of myself. I thought that I couldn't be strong in a love relationship. I even expected to be weak. It turned out, as my notes state, "that's crap." I could be strong in a love relationship. I didn't need someone else to love me in order for me to feel strong. I like to share love, and experiences, but being dependent on someone else did not make me strong. It's too bad I hadn't seen all of this many years earlier.

When I first voiced my opinion and got strong, I think it sometimes annoyed my kids and Alan. They made me feel I was wrong. I felt responsible for everything they attacked me for, so I didn't feel lovable. From their reactions, I gathered that it was wrong to be strong. It got me into trouble. It was easier to revert to being Doormat Dora.

When I felt down, angry, afraid or insecure, when I was confused, or asking what I'd done wrong, I learned I had to go to a deeper place inside myself, to think about what love is. I also had to acknowledge that when Alan did help me with things I felt strongly about, that was okay. And when he opposed me, I doubted myself, and that was mistaken. I had to learn that I could be strong without him.

I needed the nourishment of being loved, of being able to share both the lovable and the strong parts of myself. And I had to learn to ask for what I wanted and needed. To recognize it and feel it. As Harry said, if you stand firm on both feet, yourself, you will be grounded.

In one process, called the Sun Goes Down, we learned that the sun is present even in the face of dark times. If you wait until the sun comes out before you try to grow, you can stay stuck in an issue, blaming yourself and feeling bad. Instead, you have to see that the sun is still present, even if it is hidden and that love is still present, even during painful events. The mainstay is that the sun's continuing presence means that your potential to change continues.

Even when you must separate from someone, and make yourself vulnerable, envision the hurt as growing pain, and know that the sun will always rise. Instead of contention, Harry urged us to try to connect with other people with a degree of tenderness that appreciates their essence. Treating other people with awareness that they have a meaningful essence within themselves creates an atmosphere for the sun to emerge.

Affirmations

Harry taught that we don't need someone else to tell us that we are lovable, strong and capable. We have that knowledge within ourselves. He made very good use of affirmations, of telling yourself what you need to hear. In his "Aliveness Exercise," his students would state, "I am strong. I am independent. I am loving. I am caring. I see my strength."

I made this list of affirmations during his workshops: I can speak for myself. I can be strong. I can take care of myself. I can express my fears. I can cope with my fears by communicating them and not by trying to pretend they don't exist. I am not to blame for the way people speak to me. I am not responsible for other people's behavior toward me. I didn't create it. I must stop thinking that something I did was wrong. I can be calm and peaceful and content alone.

When I stated these affirmations initially, as I was learning about their power in the early 1980s, I felt that the parts of me that were not yet strong started changing. Something really began happening to me. At first, I was very scared. I clung to the security I had during my marriage. I was afraid that Alan would take it away from me. I didn't know what his next move would be, and I felt attacked and frightened, not strong at all. I had self-pitying thoughts, like what did I do to deserve this? I had given away my power to Alan by idolizing him and assuming he could do no wrong. I didn't see that for a long time.

As a therapist, I had to help withdrawn people connect to their essence, to feel the strength inside themselves. As I helped them to become grounded, to stop floating, to straighten out, to become their affirmations, I had to believe my affirmations, too. As a therapist, I could see the drama my clients experienced, and how they could get pulled down by doubting themselves. As I connected with them, I saw the power of expressing affirmation. It changes behavior.

If you state the affirmations that support who you really are, your behavior will follow your statements. Our attitudes are in our heads, but we can translate them into action. In a training exercise called "Reach for Essence," we learned to reach for the source within ourselves, to go deeper inside. Even amid conflict, have faith in yourself and reach toward that source.

Your source loves you without barriers and fear. Instead of falling into the negative parts of yourself, feel that love. Be open to your heart. You have a choice.

As you experience the qualities of openness, getting in touch with your sadness, seeing your own potential for completeness, and envisioning what it might be like to become free, you can feel a little easier and sense the light around you. Ask yourself what you need right now, envision it, ask what it would be like to have it, and then tell yourself you deserve it. When you act on your awareness, change occurs. You will begin to touch the light.

Lessons Learned

After you meet your basic needs (as outlined by Erickson in the chapter about Sid Simon), you can find your higher, spiritual self. Spirituality is wholeness, reaching your essence in wisdom, caring, and loving yourself nonjudgmentally.

Having a secret segment of your life hampers your spirituality and quest for wholeness. Recognizing and sharing your feelings is the path to finding your higher self. I learned the importance of feeling your emotions, and embracing your feelings with acceptance and serenity. As one of my class notes flatly states, "in the grieving is the healing."

Like many people, I first had to work through childhood trauma instead of keeping it buried. I had to become aware of the way I was treated as a child, being told so many negative things about myself. I believed so many ideas that put me down, that I wasn't worthwhile or strong. I had to break the cycle of my family's pattern, because my mother's mother also put her down. It was very deep in our behavior.

I see now that I was more able to break this matriarchal pattern with my son than with my daughters. I see now that I criticized them as I did myself, and I expected perfection from them, as I did from myself. Now, we've all had to learn that we have the choice to see ourselves in a loving, positive way.

Awareness is the key. I was stuck in that negativity and had to learn that I am capable—and lovable. The goal is to find that home within yourself, the deeper peace within, by being yourself and loving yourself. Unless you love yourself, it's very hard to love another person. Love is a union, a reflection of each other. In a trusting relationship, the more you give away, the more you get back. It is scary to take the risk of sharing, but love can be bigger than fear.

If you believe in yourself and accept yourself, criticism from people who are trying to undermine your self-esteem won't matter. If you accept yourself as you are, you'll also be more accepting of other people.

As early as 1980, I realized that the purpose of my life is to be willing to grow emotionally, to take that risk, to go searching to find out who I am so I could contribute my energy to helping others and share what I've learned about love.

First, I had to build the self-esteem I needed to stop burying my strength and power. I had to acknowledge that I was not living for me, but for my family. That was the case for such a long time that

I had to learn or re-learn how to live for myself. I was all wrapped up in old negative beliefs about myself. I had to learn to see myself clearly and forgive myself, to accept my positive and negative parts and integrate them.

Only then I could learn how to give in the right way, with an open hand. In that learning process, the only way out was to go through those changes. Otherwise I would have remained stuck, in a prison of fear that I created and kept my family in, or tried to keep them in. Now I support them in trying to find out who they are. I learned that my strength resides in accepting, giving and loving.

Part of my quest for finding fulfillment in myself was to learn to accept my adult children's choices and continue to love them despite long distances and different decisions. I had to learn to let go of my sense of being responsible for the people in my life, for needing to change them. First, I had to change myself. I had to see me, not as perfect, but as lovable and capable. By using the tools of personal growth, I had to learn to resist my negative parts—or subpersonalities—integrate them, believe in myself, and stop worrying about keeping up an image that mattered only to me. When I accept myself for who I am, not who my image tells me to be, I can replace hate and anger with energy and love. When I learned to give to myself—to accept that sometimes I'll succeed and sometimes I'll fail—I can be much better at giving to my children in a way that supports them in growing emotionally themselves.

I had to free myself from the image of the ideal suburban housewife, super Mom and all that. To be whole, to be a giver, I had to accept myself and break loose from the idea of perfection. By accepting myself, I became an accepting person. If I believe in myself, I can do whatever I need to do.

As I learned from Harry Sloan, we are always in the process of becoming all that we can be.

In 2016, I moved into assisted living at the Vi in Aventura, Florida. During the first week I lived there, I was seated for dinner one night with five other ladies, and I was introduced to each of them. We were all talking about our sons. A woman named Dolly was sitting next to me. She spoke of her son Harry. I quickly learned that she was Harry Sloan's mother, though we had never met before. I was white with shock, and was so pleased to get to know her. Harry himself had died—during the time we were working together—at the tragically young age of 46, some 40 years earlier. In the past five years, Dolly has become like family to me. I made a party for her, here at the Vi, for her 101st birthday. I think Harry would be pleased.

Poldi Orlando

In 1988, I began attending workshops by Poldi Orlando, PhD. My first workshop with her was "The Child Within," which explored the relationship between who we are as adults and our inner child. Poldi, who was very involved in psychosynthesis and mediation, often used art, music, movement, imagery, and ritual in her sessions. I worked with her for several years. I learned from Poldi that I am responsible for my life. I can create it. I can promote and allow whatever I want in my life to be in it—and refuse what I do not want. She was enormously affirming, teaching us to say, "I am me. No one is exactly like me. It's up to me to be open and connected to myself and what I need."

Author Steven Jay Fogel explained that although it may seem that the brain is pretty much set by adulthood, it remains malleable throughout adulthood. It continues to change as we learn and adapt. Most of us are unaware that elements of our inner child's development are constantly tugging at us, and we don't have a clue that this is happening...Our inner child responds to the emotional pain we experience and interprets it with the limited understanding we had when we were very young. It continues to steer our reactions and behavior as adults in often inappropriate ways. Awareness creates an opportunity to change. In therapy, we can gain awareness of how our adult brain can take command of the inner child, Fogel wrote.

When I was working with Poldi, it was very important for me to become more connected to myself, since I was depressed after my divorce. I had to go deeper into who I really was, amid my family, volunteer work, and studies. I had to build positive feelings about myself, instead of yielding to negative self-images or believing everyone else's reactions. I had a hard time connecting to my inner self until I learned that I had to pause and allow myself to be in touch with my negative ideas about myself that were impeding my growth.

It was important to accept myself totally, including the negative or weak parts, and instead of hiding them and hating them in myself, to see them as strengths. I had to accept my feminine side, which I thought was weak, and my male side, which I saw as my source of power—and not give that power away to the men in my life and become dependent on them. Instead, I had to integrate both sides of myself and accept myself totally, without fear.

In this process, nature became my metaphor of growth, a way to follow the instruction "go into a place where you want to be." When I walked around the island where I lived, I was surrounded by water. As a child, the movement of water was not part of my experience, even though we lived on Miami Beach, just blocks from the sea. I had too much fear of nature and water and myself. Now, I could walk alone by the water with no one telling me what to do, how to move, where to walk. I could experience the ocean's movement and feel the water on my feet. I could think about how I felt, not how I was supposed to feel. I was creating what I wanted and felt.

Poldi outlined three levels of mediation, ways of thinking things through—creative (artistic expressiveness), receptive (what you take from your past), and "reflexative." Walking by the water, I experienced what she meant by reflexative mediation, taking in my experience as it happened or, in her words, "not choosing but yet finding."

Poldi suggested reflexative mediation as a way to identify with the world around me, to see what story it wanted to tell me and what story I wanted to tell it. I learned I could take in whatever I decided to notice. She taught her students to connect with themselves, to ask "who am I?"

I found that in my diary, I answered her question with a metaphor: "I want to be like a river flowing with gentle strength and power, continuing, moving onward, not stopping or getting stuck. Its beauty and radiance stay alive in spite of the mountains, falls, and huge rocks and storms that continue to block its flow onward."

My Life Today

Before the last section of my book, which includes quotations that I want to share because I feel they have meaning for everyone, let me describe my life today.

At 89, I have a real sense of being home and being needed at the Vi. I remember when I first visited here, I was eating dinner with the sales director and saw my cousin and a lady I went to high school with in the dining room. It's been like a reunion moving here.

I have a warm circle of friends here, and my son Chayim and his family live nearby. I have found ways to be of service to others, most notably by serving as the chair of the Food & Beverage Committee as a member of the Resident Council, a position to which I was recently re-elected. It was very important to me to be a part of making sure everyone had meals and personal attention during the Covid lockdown. I was a member of the Lifestyle Committee, and I am an active participant in Torah Studies and Shabbat Services.

I have a lovely two-bedroom apartment with a big sunny porch filled with my garden of bromeliads. I have good neighbors, and we made it through the pandemic together (with an occasional masked meeting amid the quarantine to play a little Rummy Cube). As we return to more normal times, I can enjoy my friends and family here. My grandkids are such a special part of my life, and I'm so proud of them and their accomplishments. To share my family with my friends is really special.

Other than recovering from a recent fall, I am strong and well, and glad to be mentally fit as I approach my 90th birthday. I am grateful for all my experiences, all the people who have been in my life, my beloved family, and all the lessons I have learned and taught. I still check off the major markers for contentment: the ability to love, be loved, and find meaning in my daily life.

My Ethical Will

I wrote this for the end of my book. My book is my ethical will.

It tells of my hopes and aspirations, and explains my values and what my life stood for. It's all about love. God is Love, as I said on the first page. My ethical will contains the lessons I've learned through my life's experiences, my accumulated wisdom, and some tools and keys I learned along the way. I hope my children, grandchildren, and great-grandchildren will want to know these keys and tools, because they are the measure of many years of investment of time and energy.

As Rabbi Mark Kram wrote, my learning taught me the keys to enter the world of Judaism. Learning represented the importance of what I decided to do with my life: to bring my family and friends closer to God's love. Like Rabbi Kram, my final message is to remain close to your family.

MY SPIRITUAL LEADERS

Rabbi Herbert Baumgard

I have already written of how Rabbi Herbert Baumgard, the founding rabbi of Temple Beth Am, made me comfortable with asking questions and learning, even though I had been brought up to see Judaism as static and unapproachable. He taught me that I could embrace and live my faith.

As you have seen in the stories about our involvement with Temple Beth Am, he was an incomparable support and guide for those of us in volunteer leadership positions in the synagogue, and a solid spiritual guide for everyone in the congregation. He could mediate, appreciate, conciliate, and redirect with skill. I saved many of his written weekly messages over the years and want to share a selection of excerpts from some of the ones that touched me.

Rabbi Baumgard outlined some basic Jewish ideas, the core of our belief system. He begins with "God is One." And then he explains we should understand the nature of God in terms of "creation, law, justice, mercy, forgiveness" and "love." He says God is beyond man's comprehension, but is not a blind, whimsical force that acts out of anger or an urge to punish us. The Torah, he says, is our moral code, a set of laws undergirding society. Our happiness and social stability depend on learning and following this law.

He urges us to deduce a people's religiosity from their actions, not their stated beliefs, and to understand that every person is born with the potential to be good or evil, so all people can improve their character and grow as individuals by working toward a good society.

In a class in 1971, Rabbi Baumgard said that doing a mitzvah, a good deed, is doing what you don't have to do, but you know if you do it, the world or another person will benefit. Jewish philosophy believes, he said, that there is an organic relationship between peoples' deeds and the well-being of society and the world. He taught us that there are two kinds of mitzvahs. The first is an act of voluntary kindness. The second is more irrational, and is based on performing the rituals and customs that continue our communal ties. While Reform Jews do not perform as many of these rituals and customs as Orthodox Jews, they must maintain some rituals so that Reform Judaism doesn't become "a spirit without a body." Acts like lighting Shabbat candles can, he said, "be the vehicle for conveying emotion and thoughts from generation to generations, giving rituals their meaning."

To go back for a minute to his statements about Judaism's core beliefs, he said people should focus their actions on correcting the ills of this world, not on the world to come, whatever it might be. Rabbi Baumgard also included striving toward a future of peace and harmony, the "messianic day." But instead of positing that we await a Messiah, he states, "there is a part of the Messiah in all of us, and we must bring those pieces together to create God's Kingdom.

He added two more core points: First, human beings are God's co-partners in creation and are responsible for being His agents and having a sense of duty. And, second, Jews are bound to God in a special covenant; as the first to declare that God is one, they must be "exemplary in character and teach these ideas, by example, to the world."

While other teachers and scholars see some of these precepts somewhat differently, particularly Orthodox scholars, I found that Rabbi Baumgard always focused on a high moral and ethical stance, and his work and life remained consistent with these beliefs. As he wrote about our synagogue's beginnings, "Beth Am became one of the earliest Reform congregations in the country to try to blend the rationality of 'classical Reform' with the emotionality of the tradition." At the founding, this came down to some practical notes. On the question of head coverings, the clergy would also wear hats on the pulpit, but members could make their own choices. The shul kitchen, while not Kosher, would avoid forbidden foods, like pork and shellfish. It would be pro-Zionist, include some meaningful amount of Hebrew language in the liturgy, and institute Bat Mitzvahs as well as Bar Mitzvahs.

That sounds obvious now, but it was not in 1956. When Beth Am began, Kendall was mostly undeveloped, the land to its south was mostly swamp, and he was not yet the national figure he became as president of the Synagogue Council of America and Beth Am's senior rabbi.

In 1987, Rabbi Baumgard remembered attending a rabbinical council where Golda Meir was the speaker and he asked her, "Madam Prime Minister, what message would you have us take back to our congregations in America." She responded, "Tell them not to forget who they are."

He subsequently wrote in our synagogue bulletin, "In a real way

Mrs. Meir's admonition has been the basis of all my teaching for this past 30 years. I have been trying to teach you not to forget who you are, for I believe that to be a Jew is a destiny, a weighty burden, and a thrilling opportunity. To be a Jew is to be a descendant of the prophets and a bearer of the ethical law. To be a Jew is to be a descendant of slaves and the inheritor of a history of suffering and discrimination. To be a Jew is to be the child of the people who gave the world its goals of peace and justice and the faith to work toward the realization of those goals. To be a Jew is to be the beneficiary of a tradition that teaches that there is a God who cares about the lowly and the outcast, and that we have to imitate this God in His Holiness and in his caring. My message is the message I have tried to teach you for more than 30 years: 'Don't forget who you are'."

Each month, the *Beth Am Commentator* newsletter was in my mail and I learned about life from Rabbi Baumgard. I found these excerpts from his writings especially helpful and meaningful:

October 4, 1967: "How Does God Reveal Himself," Rosh Hashanah sermon

"We Jews believe that the ethical law is evidence of the reality of God.

"Judaism is an evolving and growing religion…if the Torah was thought to be a direct revelation from God, it would be very difficult to change the laws in the Torah. This became a problem when, hundreds of years after the death of Moses, Israelites lived under different conditions. They needed some additions to and changes in the laws. A group of Jews closely identified with the Temple, known as the Sadducees, said, 'You cannot change this law, for it is the direct will of God.' A group of scholarly specialists in the law, in the developing traditions of the people, known as the Pharisees, said, 'We do not wish to change the spirit of the law, but we have to change the letter of the law in order to meet the needs of the people.' The Pharisees were the compilers of the Talmud, a group of laws extending the teachings of the earlier Torah.

They were the liberals of their time, which was 2000 years ago. The Pharisees taught that if God could reveal his will to Moses on Mount Sinai, He could also reveal His will to others. The past was sacred, said the Pharisees, but not so sacred that the living needs of the people had to be neglected. The Pharisees put forth a proposition that a selected group of scholars, deeply trained in the Torah, had the right to project new laws based on the spirit of the old law. This is how the Talmud was formed, this is how Jews came to teach that the will of God can be revealed through human reason and scholarship…

It was part of the Hassidic premise that every person has a spark of the divine within him. Since this is so, the man who becomes aware of this spark of greatness within himself participates in a revelation… For Hasidim, the sounds and visions of God were everywhere, anywhere, for God was in everything…The Hasidim taught, 'Every righteous man must first learn the laws of the Torah, but then, he has the obligation to become a Torah himself, to become, though his deeds, a symbol of the divine presence."

September 1971: "Where Is the Truth," Rosh Hashanah sermon

"The Jews of old asked this question with equal fervor: Where is the truth? Where can we find it? Where can we go in search of it? Those who wrote the Torah provided an answer. The book of Deuteronomy reads, 'Do not ask who will go to heaven and get it for us? And do not ask who will cross the great sea to find it for us? For the truth is very near to you.' The ancient Jewish teachers suggested that the truth is to be found in the wisdom of the ages as distilled and spelled out in the Torah itself. Only study the Torah, our fathers taught, and you will discover ways to solve your problems and gain a purpose sufficient to sustain you through the rigors of life.

"If we define Torah as the gathered learning experience of mankind, we will have to support what the written Torah itself suggests. While the Torah clearly does not contain modern scientific knowledge, the critical student of the Torah…is constantly amazed to discover how much the scholars are old knew about the nature of man and about the recurrent problems of human society.

"One would think that those interested in acquiring knowledge would turn to the old masters for inspiration, but the great urging of many of our brightest people today is in another direction entirely. They want to experience things for themselves…[Yet] to take this position is to cast away as meaningless all the suffering of mankind up to this point, suffering through which men have learned at least some of the vital facts and rules of life. Judaism...has long taught the value of learning by doing, but this does not suggest that you cannot learn even more by observing what others have done."

September, 1973: "The Beckoning God," Rosh Hashana service

"Judaism speaks of God as a beckoner, as one who says to Israel and to man, 'Come to me; Follow me; pattern yourselves after my deeds. Be as I am.' Judaism teaches there is no mysterious or magical Salvation. To please God, we must imitate him in his goodness. The 19th chapter of Leviticus begins, 'Ye shall be holy because I the Lord your God am holy.' The chapter then includes a number of specific ways in which Jews might imitate the actions of God. Every Jew should know this chapter backwards. It includes such teachings as leaving the corners of the field to the poor, removing the stumbling block for the blind, loving your neighbor (clearly Jesus borrowed much from this chapter, and why not? He was a Jewish teacher) and loving the stranger. Judaism can be defined as that religion which teaches that man is made 'in the image of God.' It teaches that man has the potential and the obligation to grow in God's image, that is, in the image of active justice, love, and mercy.

The Hasidim of the 18th century told this story: A disciple asked his master, 'Rabbi, how is it that sometimes God seems to be so far away? The rabbi began his answer with a question: How does a father teach his child to walk? If the father always held on to the child's hand, the child would always be dependent, and he would never learn to walk. So the father steps away from the child, faces him, and beckons to him'."

January 9, 1981: "Don't We All Believe in the Same God?"

"The Jewish view of God is that He creates each of us in a pure state, that we are born in his image and the enjoins us to imitate Him in His holy deeds. Judaism teaches it is not our faith but our deeds that 'save' us…

"The deeply religious person is the one who constantly searches for the greater God…

"God is what He is regardless of our ability to understand Him in his totality."

November 21, 1986: "What Liberal Jews Believe," Yom Kipper evening service

"If you were to ask me, 'Do you believe in Heaven?', I would answer, 'of course.' But I mean something entirely different by that term than the Fundamentalists who have a very literal interpretation for it. *In a funeral eulogy, I often speak of the individual person as the river and God as the ocean.* I believe that each of us is an outlet of the divine spirit. I believe that God lives through each of us, rejoices with us, achieves with us, and suffers with us.

This analogy affected me so deeply that I have never forgotten it. I never thought of an individual person as a river and God as the ocean.

Rabbi Baumgard said that what happens to each of us is of critical importance to the world, because what happens to each of us is also happening to God. The person who lives by this faith will measure his deeds by a more exacting standard, and he will understand that he does not suffer alone. Our prayerbook says, 'God is closer than breathing.' Can this mean that the Divine and the human are part of the same essence, that eternal life is indeed within us?

In Liberal Judaism, it is possible to entertain varying theories about the unknowables like God and life after death. But if this is so, you might well ask, if it is possible to have different hypotheses, how can we believe anything at all with conviction? To this there is a simple reply. If one knows all the answers, there is no need of faith. *I believe with Einstein that we will always be as infants in comprehending the universe, and ultimately one has to make a leap of faith as to what the probabilities are and as to how one chooses to live one's life.*

February 17, 1987: "The Need for Rules and Standards"

A rabbi, like a social worker and a psychologist or psychiatrist, is in an ideal position to measure what is happening in society and to individuals. All the specialists to whom I have spoken are saying one thing—there is more unhappiness in the world with our burgeoning freedom, more desperation. All of those who deal with broken lives tend to agree. We need a return to rules and standards. We need to return to parental firmness and family loyalty.

This is not to suggest not all the rules must be exactly those administered by our parents. Some liberalizing of their standards is in order, but the present openness is sheer madness. It is also true that exceptions to rules are necessary in special situations. *But flexibility is different from license. One can be firm and loving at the same time.*

This is not an invitation for parents to be autocratic. Parents have to understand the needs of their children and encourage them to express their fears, their needs, and their opinions. *Nonetheless, parents must sometimes require their children to act in ways that the children might choose to oppose.* Teenagers especially need limitations and strong guidance. *Young people really need their parents to be parents*, that is, the models of right conduct and guides to right conduct. Sooner or later, the splits now tearing society apart will make a reverse of the current rush to hedonistic living necessary. Meanwhile, each of us must try to do what he can in his own household. *We must stand firm—with loving understanding*

May 22, 1987: "The Different God"

"How is the God of Israel different from all the other gods, that is all the ones worshipped by the ancient Semites and Egyptians? The answer is that he is the only God tied to a Torah, a moral law. When we speak of the 'holy God,' then, we are talking about the only God with a moral orientation. Today we take it for granted that God and morality are synonymous. This is a testimony to the Jewish contribution to world religious thought. We think of God and morality because the Jewish people have taught us this. The content of this morality is spelled out in detail in the history of our people. Most people call this history the Bible.

"The 19th chapter of the book of Leviticus tells us of a very specific command which God puts to Israel. God proclaims, 'You shall be holy because I the Lord your God am holy.' *This is Judaism defined. Jews are asked to imitate God in His Holiness. Jews are asked to be different just as God is different.* The Torah says that the Israelites are to be a different people, that means a morally oriented people.

The Prophet Amos (9th century BCE) teaches, "Chosenness means extra responsibility. Because God knew us first and called us to be the bearers of his moral law, we have to act in a more exalted manner than others. There are not special awards for this, declares Amos, but there are special demands upon us. The Prophet Isaiah, who lived somewhat later than Amos, tells us that God wants us to be a light unto the nations. Isaiah says Israel is God's servant. With that title and responsibility, proclaims the Prophet, goes suffering and misunderstanding, but God will cause us to prosper in the end when, "The world is filled with the knowledge of the Lord as the waters cover the sea."

"To be a Jew is a high calling. If one understands that he is a Jew in this profound sense, one does not have to find oneself. One does not have to find out who I am. To be a Jew is to be handed a lifetime of duty when you are first born. The problem is, how many modern Jews know what it is to be a Jew?

April 17, 1987: From Rabbi Baumgard's remarks at the Tribute Service honoring his work and his retirement.

The quote on our old sanctuary's wall is from the teaching of the Prophet Zechariah, which says, *"Not by military power, nor by force, but by My spirit,"* saith the Lord. Alan and I donated the installation of that message, and we were moved that the Rabbi quoted it in his remarks at the Tribute Service honoring his leadership of our synagogue when he retired. After he quoted that statement, Rabbi Baumgard continued:

"I leave behind that legacy. From the first window on the right of the sanctuary, we also read this teaching from our prayerbook, 'Each day God recreate the deeds of creation." I leave behind that message of hope. And from the window on my right, there calls the teachings of Rabbi Hillel, who said, *'If I am not for myself, who is for me, but if I am for myself alone, what am I? And if not now, when?'* I leave behind this challenge to caring action. Indeed, since I am responsible for choosing all of these messages from our tradition, seen on our windows, I will, in a sense, never cease speaking in this beautiful Sanctuary.

"You see, I have tricked you, for I have encapsulated the great messages of our tradition here in the Sanctuary. They are mine, yes, simply because I have tried to make them my own. *They are not only the legacy of our tradition, they are in a smaller but more immediate sense, my gift to you. My prayer is that each of you will make them your message as well. I pray that each of you will come to possess these teachings and give them in turn to others.*

"I want you to know that…here at Beth Am…we have done all this together… We have shared over these 30 years not just the construction of half a dozen buildings, nor just the development of important spiritual and moral programs. What we have shared is half a lifetime."

When I heard these words, I was very fulfilled and happy to realize that our family was an integral part of those 30 years and the career of this excellent leader and teacher.

What If You Fail?

You and I know that some of the nicest people we know are not a financial success, yet the thrust of our society seems to demean these splendid people. How are they to hold their heads high—unless they have something many of the successful people don't have—a spiritual orientation towards life, a value orientation towards people.

Many a person who has made it financially suddenly discovers that he seems to have failed in life. His marriage may break up, a child may be seriously injured, his business might be sold from underneath him, he might lose the respect of his professional comrades, old friends may for some reason turn away-- suddenly the perfect life falls into fragments, and the person asks for the first time, What is it all about? How could I, always successful, suddenly be a victim of circumstances?

A Rabbi is in the position to observe not only the successes but the failures in life. He notes that almost no one is a success at all phases of his life. Sooner or later we all become the victims, even if it is delayed until old age when the quality of our life becomes diluted by illness.

Those who know denial and defeat early in their life are sometimes able to cope with blows later in life better than those who have always had it easy. It is a talent to learn how to deal with these blows. It is a blessing, maybe the greatest blessing.

Trouble comes to everyone. The only difference between us is how we deal with the trouble. Some are able to float like a boat on a stormy sea. Others sink beneath the waves but bob upward after asserting their will to conquer their problems. He who has learned how to rise above a failure of a sort has learned a great deal and can be a teacher to many.

How does the prayer in our prayer book go? We know not, Oh Lord, whether the gifts for which we ask are for our good, whether our trials and tribulations may not be blessings in disguise, whether even the fragment of our shattered hopes and loves may not minister to the upbuilding of other lives and the fulfillment of Your unfathomable

plan... Teach us to face life with faith and courage that we may convert sorrow and struggle into blessings...
(Note: this was so good! Very informative about life!)

Excerpts from a High Holiday Sermon

By Rabbi Dr. Herbert M. Baumgard, Temple Beth Am, Miami, FL

While Judaism has long taught that the soul returns to God at death, Jewish mourning ceremonies do not stress this theological doctrine. What is stressed is the agony and the mystery of human separation. What our ceremonies try to deal with are sorrow and loneliness. In other words, Judaism directs its main attention to those who survive.

We set aside a full week for the ceremony of Shivah, where those who have lost a loved one are encouraged to sit at home while their friends come to commiserate with them. If you are angry, say so. If you feel guilty, say so. None of these feelings are considered to be anti-religious or opposed to religious practice. On the contrary, they are considered to be normal feelings and if they exist, as they do in most people, it is better for them to be expressed.

God Himself weeps.

I believe in a God who shares our sorrows and grieves with us. After all, this is the kind of God who spoke to Moses out of the Burning Bush—when He said, I have heard the cry of my people.

I see their suffering; I know their pain.

If you are filled with grief, it is important not to hide it. You should not pretend that nothing has happened. The psychologists tell us that grief, if bottled up in the present, will explode at some future time. How wise the ancient Rabbis were to establish a required period when mourners are to be at home and to acknowledge with their friends the great tragedy that has taken place!

When someone close to you dies, there is usually a feeling that a part of you has died also. If we are the parents, a part of our future seems to die with the child. If we are the children, a part of our supporting foundation seems to die with the parent. There is definitely a loss of ego when someone in the family dies. Judaism tries to recognize this fact and urges the mourner to move closer at this time to the rest of his family and to the Jewish community. The kaddish ceremony, which requires that the mourner come to the synagogue on a regular basis following a death, is based on this psychological truth. As the mourner says his kaddish along with others, he realizes that he is not alone in his sorrow and that he is a part of an ongoing community from which he can borrow strength.

While we encourage deep mourning at a time of death, we believe that continued morning should not become a way of life. Such living, our tradition teaches, is a denial of God and a closing of one's eyes to life's opportunities. It is not easy, however, to redirect oneself towards new people when a loved one with whom we have lived closely for many years passes away.

When you have difficulty releasing your sorrow, you should make certain to reach out to others for help. Of course, we would rather talk about other living things, but it is important to learn that death is a part of life. We are born to die, and as a members of our congregation get older, more of us can be expected each year to pay this price for the privilege of living. The mature person will want to face the inevitable prospect of death, so that he can plan his life more meaningfully. By accommodating oneself to the sure prospect of a future death, one can live with less anxiety, and you might decide to live more slowly and to smell the flowers along the way. If we can become more objective about what we are doing, chances are we will be more at peace and more content.

The contemplation of death ought to give us an extra field of perception. The truth is that our name lives on only in terms of what we add to the life of others. Our name lives on with our children and with the things that we give away—with the deeds that we do to enrich the lives of others and with the gifts that we contribute to make the lives of others easier and fuller. Let us think about the inevitability of our death and resolve to live in such a way that when that moment arrives, it will find us confident that we have made of this life what we could and what we should.

One of the most important things Rabbi Baumgard did for me was to suggest that I read *Man's Search for Meaning* by Dr. Viktor Frankl. In this book, Dr. Frankel writes about everything he learned as a prisoner in a Nazi concentration camp. As a social worker and as someone trained in many psychological approaches, I found his writing very meaningful, both his memoir and his teachings about Logo Therapy, which he invented while a prisoner. A neurologist and psychiatrist, Frankl based his approach on the idea that a person's primary motivation is to find meaning in life.

In his book, I learned about tolerance. You must find your own conscious answers to life's up and downs. We have no control. We must find that place in our own spiritual convictions. Frankl firmly believed that our inner world is as real as our outer world, so we must uncover our inner world.

Life is about love. Don't worry about what is going to happen. You must live in the moment. Take action in the moment. Having a great relationship with yourself is a good way to live. But, how can we take care of ourselves? We all have a choice. How can we distinguish our inner voice? Ask yourself: What are you feeling right now? Without this inner voice, we have a lack of freedom. To get to it, we must stand on our own feet and take action without fear.

When you want to find a passion that can make you survive whatever horrors happen in your life—and, remember, he was in Auschwitz—*you have to get to that place of love inside yourself. You must deal with your anger and resentment. While you never forget, you must forgive for your own sake.* "We are here to love and learn."

Frankl learned that taking care of others gave his time in the concentration camp meaning. *He urges his readers to make responsible choices.* To become a loving, giving person, show kindness in life. We are here to help or to learn. Frankl learned to be more respectful in his life and to stay in the moment. Helping people (others) gives meaning to our lives.

It was amazing to me how I had to learn to make responsible choices as an adult, and I urge young people to heed Frankl's message: *"Consider if it is good for you, and then do it, and if it's not, don't do it."*

I learned this concept from my psychologist Dr. Marquit when I was in my 30's. And I built on it after reading Frankl's book. You can find that place inside yourself to be happy. I learned that when we choose to be happy, happiness will come. As Abraham Lincoln said, "People are as happy as they tell themselves they are."

Rabbi Kalman Packouz

Starting in 1970, I began receiving the weekly Shabbat Shalom fax from Aish HaTorah. It was written by the late Rabbi Kalman Packouz. I saved them to read again and again, and finally gave most of my collection to Rabbi Smith at the Vi, who found them very inspiring.

Rabbi Packouz's personal warmth and wisdom came through in everything he wrote and taught. In one newsletter, he said, "Learning Torah is the heart, soul, and lifeblood of the Jewish people. It is the secret of our survival. Learning leads to understanding and understanding leads to doing. One cannot love what he does not know. Learning Torah gives you the joy of understanding life." As it says in Proverbs, "The most important thing is that the study of Torah is our most sacred obligation."

In 1996, he wrote, "What does God want of you? Only that you remain in awe of God, your Lord, so that you will follow all His paths and love Him. Serving God, your Lord, with all your heart and with all your soul, you must keep his commandments and decrees so that all good will be yours."

As he said, "There are two ways to fail: do without thinking and think without doing."

Whatever you decide to do, whatever action you take, he believed, worrying was not useful. In one issue of the Shabbat Shalom fax he quoted Rabbi Chaim Shmelevitz on that subject: "A person creates his own mental torture by his own thoughts. If you keep worrying about the future, you will never have Peace of Mind. Regardless of what will be next year, you're causing yourself suffering right now!"

"One's self image is a key factor in one's behavior. Moses's self-image was of a prince growing up in the palace of an absolute monarch. This allowed him to take any action necessary to do what was right."

Each holiday, the Shabbat Shalom fax provided words of wisdom and thoughts to ponder.

When he wrote about the holiday of Succoth, for example, he said, "Living in a Succah puts life into perspective. Our history has borne this out. No matter if we have established wealth and security, in the end a dwelling is temporary. Our trust must be in God. The key to Jewish survival, better yet, the key to Judaism, is education. The children must see their parents learning and living Judaism in the home.

On Yom Kippur, Rabbi Packouz said to think about these three questions:

1. Am I eating to live or living to eat?

2. If you're eating to live, what are you living for?

3. What would you like written in your obituary or on your tombstone? That is, can you encapsulate the purpose of your life?

He wrote, "What is the essence of Yom Kippur and how do we observe it? Yom Kippur signifies that the Almighty forgave the Jewish people for the transgression of the golden calf. This day was decreed to be a day of forgiveness for our mistakes. This refers to transgressions against God. Transgressions against our fellow man require us to correct our mistakes and seek forgiveness."

The festival of Shavous—the celebration that commemorates God giving the Torah on Mt. Sinai to the whole Jewish people—is a time of rededication and commitment to learning Torah. The Torah is the lifeblood of the Jewish people. Our enemies have always known that only when we stop learning Torah, our assimilation is inevitable. Without knowledge, there is no commitment. Once cannot love what he does not know. A person cannot understand or do what he has never learned.

Rabbi Packouz campaigned against intermarriage, because he believed it damaged the structure of Jewish family life. His first book was *How to Prevent an Intermarriage*, and he had the same editor I have for this book! He warned young couples that they had to remain aware of the difference between love and infatuation. He wrote, *"Love is the pleasure of seeing virtue. Infatuation is blind.* It is the state you are in when your emotions prevent you from seeing the entire picture. *Love is not blind! It is wide-eyed. Infatuation is blind. If you think the other person is perfect, watch out!"*

When people had moral questions, he would advise strengthening their Jewish identity in the search for greater security and wisdom. He said each individual has to ask a pivotal question: "Am I facing toward the Torah or against it? Do I want to grow in my understanding and fulfillment of the Torah, or do I want to assimilate and disappear as a Jew? Do I have a heritage and a treasure to be enjoyed and shared with my children? Or will I ignore it?"

He taught, "One has to make conscious real decisions about what it means to be a Jew, how to ensure that you grow and understand the Torah, how to ensure that the next generation will be a link in the 150 generations of the Jewish people."

Parents also should make sure, he wrote, "that their young children show respect toward them and others. *If a young child forms the habit of being disrespectful to his parents or other adults, he will also lack respect for others when he grows up."*

The most precious gift you can bestow on any child is a positive self-image, Rabbi Packouz believed. Constant criticism hurts somebody's peace of mind, especially a child's. A child growing up with inferiority feelings is handicapped and will be limited in many ways. The key focus of anyone dealing with children must be, *"How can I elevate this child's self-image."*

Rabbi Packouz clearly understood how Judaism believes people should act, and he made that clear in his writings. *He defined charity, "tzedakah," as "fulfilling God's will."* This including helping someone become a better person. "The more you elevate someone else, the more he will share his high ideals with his family and other people." *When you do even a small act of kindness,"* Rabbi Packouz wrote, *"you will feel the joy of growth."*

"It is never too late to start learning about Torah," he would reassure people who were new to Torah study. "It is our heritage and the secret to happiness and fulfillment."

"Starting to learn something new as an adult is a risk," but Rabbi Packouz warned that *"the person who risks nothing, has nothing, is nothing. He may avoid pain or sorrow, but he doesn't learn, grow, or live in love. He is only a slave, chained by safety, locked away by fear."* Only a person who is willing to take a risk not knowing the results is truly alive!

Rabbi Packouz was known for his warm smile and his, short pithy messages, like: *"Kindness is a hard thing to give away—it usually comes back."*

Or, *"There are three prerequisites for happiness: someone to love, something to do, and something to look forward to!"*

Each issue of his Shabbat Shalom fax started with a meaningful story, like this one, which is called "The Present."

"Imagine life as a game in which you are juggling five balls in the air. You name them work, family, health, friends and spirit, and you're keeping all these balls in the air. You will soon understand that *work is a rubber ball; if you drop it, it will bounce back. But the other four balls—family, health, friends and spirit—are made of glass. If you drop one of these, it will be irrevocably scuffed, marked, nicked, damaged, or even shattered.* It will never be the same.

"You must understand this and strive for balance in your life. How? Don't undermine your worth by comparing yourself with others. It is because we are different that each of us is special. Don't set your goals by what other people deem important. *Only you know what is best for you.* Don't take for granted the things closest to your heart. Cling to them as you would your life, for without them life is meaningless.

"Don't let your life slip through your fingers by living in the past or for the future. By living your life one day at a time, you live all the days of your life. Don't give up when you still have something to give. Nothing is really over until the moment you stop trying. Don't be afraid to admit that you are less than perfect. It is this fragile thread that binds us to each other. Don't be afraid to encounter risks. It is by taking chances now we learn how to be brave.

> *"Don't shut love out of your life by saying it's impossible to find. The quickest way to receive love is to give; the fastest way to lose love is to hold it too tightly; and the best way to keep love is to give it wings. Don't run through life so fast that you forget not only where you have been, but also where you are going. Don't forget that a person's greatest emotional need is to feel appreciated and to give love to one's family. Don't be afraid to learn. Knowledge is weightless, a treasure you can always carry easily. Don't use time or words carelessly. The hurtful things you say cannot be taken back. Neither time nor words can be retrieved. Life is not a race, but a journey to be savored each step of the way.*

"Yesterday is history, tomorrow is a mystery, and today is a gift: that's why we call it the present."

Quotations

When you ask what makes a quote good, notice the value the quote honors or supports. Ask how you can apply it to your life in a small, actionable way, sparking reflection and awareness. A quote in and of itself isn't going to change anything without being connected to some action. You hear people talk about proverbs being handed down from generation to generation as wisdom. Sayings have long served as a way to communicate wisdom in teaching and in conversation.

When you find yourself particularly moved by a quote, inspirational, sorrowful, or otherwise, therapist Jaqueline Socastro, LCSWR, says it is important to get curious about what the words are making you feel exactly, because they could be pointing toward an opportunity for change. She recommends asking yourself, Why does this quote resonate so much with me?

Todd Thrash, a professor specializing in spirituality at William and Mary College, said, What makes a quote good is not just positivity, but who the person reading it is, what they're doing with their life, and how they're understanding the world.

I wrote this meditation as the beginning of giving myself unconditional love. It reminded me of a new behavior I was learning:

Not Being a Victim.

I used to believe other people had these behaviors, and they should give them to me. I took all the alternatives I learned and then, I gave them to me, instead. It's giving to myself.

I was never taught to give to myself. I thought my job was to give to others. I need to be reprogrammed and constantly reminded to give to myself this unconditional love!

I had to be in touch with my own power so that I didn't need a protector.

I had to believe I was lovable before I could be able to love again, and I had to be able to be loved in the other person's way, not only my way.

I had to allow it, knowing that love doesn't have to be only my way!

The risk and fear I felt about sharing these my thoughts were about how simple they are, and that perhaps they aren't important to other people.

But to me, it's all about giving to myself.

I need to constantly relearn to give myself this unconditional love.

I can give it to others.

These are quotes that I learned from wise people and collected over 50 years. I can't tell you who said them anymore, but I want to share their wisdom with you.

Love relationships are the most important part of our lives. The intimacy that is desired doesn't come from one-night stands, but from the depths of someone who knows who he or she is and what they want for themselves. Cruising bars to find such a person is difficult because the atmosphere isn't conducive to sharing and caring. Someone who is able to share an intimate relationship is a person who feels good enough about themselves to take care of themselves. Taking care of yourself enables you to share with other people in search of themselves and to take different directions.

You never know how you can change someone's life by showing you care! If we take time to care about people, each of us has something to give.

We don't quarrel with feelings. Feelings just are ours. We don't attack feelings. That's how you learn to express your deep feelings.

We are like trees. We must create new leaves, new directions, in order to grow.

I wish we could teach this message to our children: Winning is not about the gold medal, it is about the chance to do something you love. Winning is about trying and if you fail, trying again. The most precious lesson any of us can ever learn is not about winning—it is about what to do when you don't. That is the lesson more precious than gold.

All of us need to learn sometime in our lives, It doesn't matter who you are; it's what you do. The younger you are, the better!

Two things have had a huge impact on my life. Pull yourself up by your bootstraps, and it's not what happens to you, it's how you react to it.

Your future depends on the consequences of the choices you make in your life.

The two most important days in your life are the day you were born and the day you find out why,

Humility teaches me that I don't know everything, that I'm not the most important person. If you don't listen, you're not going to learn anything.

If we spent even a small percentage of the time we devote to obsessing about those we consider our rivals, competitors and enemies on examining where our own faults are, it's hard to believe we wouldn't be more successful—or at least less likely to be done in by our chief rivals hiding inside us.

It is not the number of hills that you try to climb, but the one that you get over that counts.

Meditating for 10 minutes a day lowers levels of the stress hormone (cortisol). Break a sweat exercising 30 minutes a day, provides protection against diabetes, heart problems, and dementia.

What's the most important thing you've ever learned? As teachers, we can make or break a child's life in a day or in a moment by the way we react to a situation.

The most important relationship in life is the one you have with yourself. And if you have that, then any relationship is a plus and not a must.

When you set goals for yourself, they work in two ways: you work on them and they work on you!

Real difficulties can be overcome. It's the imaginary ones that are usually insurmountable!

My favorite words of wisdom: You cannot control other people, only yourself. *You are not responsible for other people's behavior, only your own.*

Every day of your life is a choice. You can choose to have a bad day and complain about everything, or you can choose to have a good day and find the good in things.

Grant that I may not so much seek to be consoled as to console, to be understood as to understand, to be loved as to love.

For it is in giving that we receive.

It is in pardoning that we are pardoned.

It is in dying that we are born to eternal life.

When you lose your integrity, you have nothing that matters. It's downhill all the way.

Baseball Is Similar to Life (from a former major league baseball coach)

You start out at home and get a little older. (First Base)

Then in early adulthood (Second Base), you're the furthest away from home you will ever be. You get a little older and wiser (Third Base) and you see home plate, then you realize that where you want to be is where you already are.

Try not to worry about the future because you have control only over this minute.

Remember three top values: Keep God first. Be active. Do work that makes you feel good.

A grandmother's wisdom can make an invaluable influence in her grandchildren's lives.

Your future depends on the consequences of the choices you make in your life!

Engaging in positive internal dialogue is actually a mark of mental health.

I read once about a famous woman who said, "The trick of life is to keep moving."

A woman's work is measured by her children.

The five pillars of brain health: move (exercise), relax (sleep enough and avoid stress), nourish (eat well), discover (think), and connect (socialize)

3 Ways You Can Work to Put Time on Your Side (outsmart aging)

1. **Spend 20 minutes outside.** Spending time in nature each day can lower stress hormones by 20% an hour.

2. **Pencil in a brisk walk.** Moving for 30 minutes daily may help you live 10 years longer.

3. **Eat fish twice a week.** Mediterranean diet rich in Omega 3. You can get Omega 3 from walnuts, chia seeds and flax seeds.

A life has three parts: You spend one-third of your life learning, one-third of your life earning, and one-third of your life returning. *(I heard this wise saying once, and I want to repeat it to you. I have spent the majority of my senior years helping others. All religions teach us that each one of us has a responsibility to help others. The more fortunate you have been in your life, the larger the responsibility.)*

It is the human situation to meet the present with interpretations of the past. The meaning of the present is to allow us to leave the past and see the now in its own right. Experience will soon become your past and a foundation for a new present and future.

In real love, you want only good for that person. In romantic love, you want that person.

Repeat each day:

I am improving every day.
I am growing every day.
I am becoming wiser every day.
I am becoming more mature.
I am learning to relax.
I am developing greater self-confidence.
I believe in myself
I am developing greater peace of mind.
I couldn't be happier.
I am happier

The choice prizes that life has to offer go to those who make plans. Leftovers go to the aimless. Forget yesterday. Live for today. When you wake up tomorrow morning, start your new day with the conviction that happiness is but a way of living and that you love and hold the key to happiness.

We may lose it sometimes in our lives, swimming in the river of life. But we can connect and reconnect by reaching for the God within us. Not only changing other people's lives but changing our own lives from God's teachings that are in all of us—we must allow it. *Hardest thing we can do is to learn to allow it.*

It's all coming from forgiving ourselves. We can love other people but it all comes from loving ourselves.

Communication solves problems. Fighting does not solve problems. After the fight, the problem is still there. Try to communicate about the problem—that's one way of solving problems.

You don't share music with people you don't like. Singing is an intimate form of sharing. Music, Jewish mystics say, is the music of the soul. Souls have a way of understanding each other.

Thoughts to Share

Express our minds to those who may not think precisely like we do. We must open our hearts and then we discover at least the possibility of common ground.

—President Barrack Obama

I tell friends, until you are content by yourself, you won't find love. You'll be searching too hard for it.

—Julianna Margulies

Once you learn how to die, you learn how to live. So what's the secret to life? It's simple: to live every moment of your life fully with the greatest love.

—Tuesdays with Morrie

Life is not what happens to you, but what you do with what happens to you.

—Dorothy Rodham to Chelsea Clinton

Complaining about a problem without posing a solution is called whining.

—Teddy Roosevelt

It's important to listen. Most people just want to know that they are heard.

—Anne Meara

Difficulties are opportunities for inner growth.

—Maria Shriver

With all my heart now and forever, let us be grateful to people who make us happy. They are charming gardeners who make our souls blossom.

—Inscribed on a bench at the Morikami gardens.

Perhaps love (and you can substitute education if you want to) is the process of my leading you gently back to yourself. Not to whom I want you to be, but to who you are.

—Antoine de Saint-Exupéry

This is the 50th item on a list of life mistakes: Neglecting your house of worship——Women who get out to attend religious services at least once a week have a 20% reduced risk of death, regardless of whether they smoke, drink or exercise, says a study of more than 92,000 women by Yeshiva University and Albert Einstein College of Medicine. Researchers credit the emotional support and respite from stress that going to regular services can provide. Amen to that.

—Readers Digest

We have met the enemy and he is us.

—Pogo

As my compatriot Socrates told us all those centuries ago, the unexamined life is not worth living.

—Arianna Huffington

We control the climate and weather in a classroom every day, and we can choose to make it a sunny day or not.

—Haim Ginott (paraphrased)

The Dash
For it matters not how much we own
The car—the house—the cash—
What matters is how we live and love
And how we spend our Dash.

—Linda Ellis

Despite our differences, we're all alike. Beyond identities and desire, there is a common core of self—an essential humanity whose nature is peace and whose expression is thought and whose action is unconditional love. When we identify with that inner core, respecting and honoring it in others as well as ourselves, we experience healing in every area of life.

—Joan Borysenko, *Minding the Body, Mending the Mind*

We use quotes to pass on value and life lessons and also to connect and commiserate with one another.

—Hoda Kolb

Learn the word that improves your life: The more I say, Yes, the more variety there is in my life. Do I want to see a play? Yes. Do I want to take a trip? Yes. I force myself to say Yes because brain health and physical health are directly tied to novelty and change. Every time I've said Yes, it's paid off.

—Rick Foster, *Happiness and Health*

Stupid is what stupid does.

—Forest Gump

The opposite of love is not hate; it's indifference.

—Elie Wiesel, writer and
Holocaust survivor

How can you move someone else forward?

—The mantra of tennis champion Arthur Ashe, quoted at the 1968 Open

Flatter me and I may not believe you
Criticize me, and I may not like you.
Ignore me, and I may not forgive you.
Encourage me, and I may not forget you.

—William Arthur

Life has a way of breaking a person,
but that broken part makes you stronger.

—Ernest Hemingway

People are as happy as they tell themselves they are.

—Abraham Lincoln (*We can choose to be happy. That's when happiness will come. Find that place inside yourself to be happy.*)

Your 80's will be your best years.

— Oliver Sacks, *The Joy of Turning 80*

Out of clutter, find simplicity. From discord find harmony. In the middle of difficulty, lies opportunity.

—Albert Einstein

If you try to bury feelings, you bury them live. They don't die.

—John Powell

Everyone has the power for greatness—not for fame, but greatness, because greatness is determined by service!

—Oprah Winfrey

How can you serve your way to greatness? When you shift your focus from success to service. Real success means creating a life of meaning through service that fulfils your reason for being here. If you don't know what your Passion is, realize that one reason for your existence on Earth is to find it! Do what you love, give it back in the form of service, and you will do more than succeed, you will triumph!

—Oprah Winfrey

So long as you're still worried about what others think of you, you are owned by them. Only when you require no approval from outside yourself can you be your own self.

—Oprah Winfrey

Dost thou love life? Then do not squander time
for that is the stuff that life is made of.

—Benjamin Franklin

Only those who have the patience to do simple things perfectly will acquire the skill to do difficult things easily.

—Schiller

Knowledge planted in youth gives shade in old age

—Anon

You can't avoid trouble but when it comes
you needn't give it a seat to sit on.

—Reader's Digest

Ultimately, you have nothing to prove to anyone but yourself. That is what it truly means to live without fear—to keep reaching for your fullest potential.

—Neale D. Walsch

Three things in human life are important. First is to be kind. The second is to be kind and the third is to be kind.

—Henry James (reportedly said this to his nephew)

Old age is a time to counsel the young, to help the troubled, to comfort the lonely, the sick and needy. The more meaning you have found in life, the clearer will be the meaning of old age.

—John LaFarge

Expect much, you will obtain much!
Expect little, you will obtain little!
Expect nothing, you will obtain nothing!
For he that expects nothing will not be disappointed, but he that expects much—if he lives and uses that in hand day by day by day—shall be full to running over.

—Edgar Cayce

The common enemy is the nihilist, the egotist, the cynic who places himself first and all the others nowhere. I don't think God cares much if we believe in him as long as we display love of our fellow man.

—Sidney Harris

The greatest of faults is to be conscious of none.

—Carlyle

Be not merely good; be good for something.

—Thoreau

You can't change what you don't acknowledge.

—Dr. Phil McGraw

Your mind is what your brain does for a living

—Steven Jay Fogel

The Tao of Pooh

How can you get very far, if you don't know who you are? How can you do what you ought, if you don't know what you've got? And if you don't know which to do of all the things in front of you, Then what you'll have when you are through Is just a mess without a clue of all the best that can come true If you know What and Which and Who.

—Benjamin Hoff

Poems

I copied this for my English class in 10th grade from an anthology of poems. Now I think it is about the yarmulke that I found in my walker from my husband Bill Saltzman. He died 15 years ago, but I believe he put it in my walker to remind me of his love. I believe he did this.

The Token
sonnet by John Donne

Send me some token, that my hope may live,
Or that my easeless thoughts may sleep and rest;
Send me some honey to make sweet my hive,
That in my passions I may hope the best.
I beg no ribbon wrought with thine own hands,
To knit our loves in the fantastic strain
Of new-touched youth; nor ring to show the stands
Of our affection, that as that's round and plain,
So should our loves meet in simplicity;
No, nor the corals which thy wrist enfold,
Laced up together in congruity,
To show our thoughts should rest in the same hold;
No, nor thy picture, though most gracious,
And most desired, because best like the best;
Nor witty lines, which are most copious,
Within the writings which thou hast addressed.
Send me nor this, nor that, to increase my store,
But swear thou think'st 'I love thee,' and no more.

This Is The True Joy

George Bernard Shaw

This is the true joy in life, the being used for a
purpose recognized by yourself as a mighty one; the being
a force of nature instead of a feverish, selfish little
clod of ailments and grievances complaining that the world
will not devote itself to making you happy.
I am of the opinion that my life belongs to the whole
community, and as long as I live it is my privilege to do
for it whatever I can.
I want to be thoroughly used up when I die, for the
harder I work the more I live. I rejoice in life for its
own sake. Life is no 'brief candle' for me. It is a sort
of splendid torch which I have got hold of for the moment,
and I want to make it burn as brightly as possible before
handing it on to future generations.

The Rosebud

Pastor Darryl L. Brown

It is only a tiny rosebud
A flower of God's design;
But I cannot unfold the petals
With these clumsy hands of mine
The secret of unfolding flowers
Is not known to such as I
The flower God opens so gently
In my hands would fade and die
If I cannot unfold a rosebud,
This flower of God's design,
How can I have wisdom
To unfold this life of mine?

So I'll trust in Him for His leading
Each moment of every day,
And I'll look to Him for His guidance
Each step of the pilgrim way
For the pathway that lies before me
My heavenly Father knows
I'll trust Him to unfold the moments
Just as he unfolds the rose

At Days End

John Hall

Is anyone happier because you passed his way?
Does anyone remember that you spoke to him today?
The day is almost over, and its toiling time is through;
Is there anyone to utter now a kindly word of you?
Can you say tonight, in parting with the day that's slipping fast,
That you helped a single brother of the many that you passed?
Is a single heart rejoicing over what you did or said;
Does the man whose hopes were fading, now with courage look ahead?
Did you waste the day or lose it, was it well or sorely spent?
Did you leave a trail of kindness, or a scar of discontent?
As you close your eyes in slumber, do you think that God will say:
"You have earned one more tomorrow by the work you did today."

Love

Leo Rostens

Those who do not know fear are not really brave
We think much less than what we know
We know much less than what we love
We love much less than what there is
And to this precise extent we are much less than what we are.

Look Closer

Phyllis McCormack

What do you see, nurses, what do you see?
What are you thinking, when you look at me,
A crabbit old woman, not very wise,
Uncertain of habit, with far-away eyes,
Who, quite unresisting, lets you do as you will,
With bathing and feeding the long day to fill.
Is that what you're thinking, is that what you see?
Then open your eyes nurse, you aren't looking at me.
I'll tell you who I am as I sit here so still,
As I move at your bidding, as I eat at your will.
I'm a small child of 10 with a father and mother,
Brothers and sisters, who loved one another.
A bride now at 20 my heart gives a leap,
Remembering the vows that I promised to keep.
At 25 now I have young of my own,
Who need me to build a secure happy home,
At 50 once more babies play around my knee,
Again we know children, my loved one and me.
Dark days are upon me, my husband is dead,
I look at the future, I shudder with dread,
For my young are all busy with young of their own,
And I think of the years and the love that I've known.
I'm an old woman now and nature is cruel.
It's her jest to make old age look like a fool.
The body it crumbles, grace and vigor depart,
There is now a stone where I once had a heart,
But inside this old carcass, a young girl still dwells,
And now and again my battered heart swells.
I remember the joys, I remember the pain,
And I'm loving and living life over again.

I think of the years all too few gone too fast,
And accept the stark fact that nothing can last.
So open your eyes, nurse, open and see,
Not a crabbit old woman. Look closer—see me.

If

Rudyard Kipling

If you can keep your head when all about you
Are losing theirs and blaming it on you;
If you can trust yourself when all men doubt you,
But make allowance for their doubting too:
If you can wait and not be tired by waiting,
Or, being lied about, don't deal in lies,
Or being hated don't give way to hating,
And yet don't look too good, nor talk too wise;
If you can dream —and not make dreams your master;
If you can think —and not make thoughts your aim,
If you can meet with Triumph and Disaster
And treat those two impostors just the same:.
If you can bear to hear the truth you've spoken
Twisted by knaves to make a trap for fools,
Or watch the things you gave your life to, broken,
And stoop and build 'em up with worn-out tools;
If you can make one heap of all your winnings
And risk it on one turn of pitch-and-toss,
And lose, and start again at your beginnings,
And never breathe a word about your loss:
If you can force your heart and nerve and sinew
To serve your turn long after they are gone,
And so hold on when there is nothing in you
Except the Will which says to them: "Hold on!"
If you can talk with crowds and keep your virtue,

Or walk with Kings —nor lose the common touch,
If neither foes nor loving friends can hurt you,
If all men count with you, but none too much:
If you can fill the unforgiving minute
With sixty seconds' worth of distance run,
Yours is the Earth and everything that's in it,
And which is more: you'll be a Man, my son!

Success

Ralph Waldo Emerson

To laugh often and much;
to win the respect of the intelligent people
and the affection of children;
to earn the appreciation of honest critics
and endure the betrayal of false friends;
to appreciate beauty;
to find the best in others;
to leave the world a bit better
whether by a healthy child, a garden patch,
or a redeemed social condition;
to know that one life has breathed easier
because you lived here.
This is to have succeeded.

How Do I Love Thee?

To my children, grandchildren and great-grandchildren

Elizabeth Barrett Browning

How do I love thee? Let me count the ways.
I love thee to the depth and breadth and height
My soul can reach, when feeling out of sight
For the ends of being and ideal grace.
I love thee to the level of every day's

Most quiet need, by sun and candle-light.
I love thee freely, as men strive for right.
I love thee purely, as they turn from praise.
I love thee with the passion put to use
In my old griefs, and with my childhood's faith.
I love thee with a love I seemed to lose
With my lost saints. I love thee with the breath,
Smiles, tears, of all my life; and, if God choose,
I shall but love thee better after death.

Meaningful Passages

Gratitude

Gratitude reminds you of the wonders around you: the warmth of the sun, the glow of the moon and stars, the current of a river, the ripples of a lake, the waves of an ocean, the comfort of a breeze, the colors of flowers, the majesty of tall trees, the utility of buildings, the speed of planes, and the power of trains. Be grateful for the miracles of nature and the wonderous products of man; strengthen your bridge.... When you let gratitude remind you every day of the abundance in your life—your relationships, your strengths, your achievements and everything miraculous and powerful around you, you make stronger your bridge to your best possible life.

—David J. Pollay

A Grateful Letter

I wrote this letter to our beloved dog, Gigi, in December, 1983, as part of a Humanist Seminar. First, I listed her wonderful qualities: She was small and protective; she gave our family all her love; she gave us a sense of security; she was a real friend, the most reliable friend in the world; and you could always talk to her.

> *Dearest Gigi,*
> *You gave so much to our family for 14 years. You were a constant source of love to each of my children. You were always available for loving. You went from one to the other. You helped them learn how*

to love all through their stages of growth. You seemed to belong to each child solely as if you were their best friend as each one grew up! I appreciate your endless giving and sometimes wished I were you, with the amount of love Pam, Susie and Robbi constantly gave you. You're not with me and the children now, but you're always in our hearts!!

Anyone can make a difference in anyone's life.

Each one of us must climb alone to the top of our own mountain and have a conversation with God. We need to reflect on our lives and ask ourselves, Have I been living a full and righteous life? Am I making a difference, even a small one, in this world? Have I given freely of my heart and have I touched others with my goodness and generosity? These questions and so many more we can find around us as we grow and find fulfillment in our lives.

The older I get, the more comfortable I become with taking risks. Sometimes I get overwhelmed coping with things, but experience has taught me how to manage. When you get older, you lose so much. Experience at falling and getting up. You're not going to stop falling. But you will get better at getting up and brushing yourself off. I believe that. I lived it.

We create. We promote and we allow everything that happens in our lives.

I learned I want to share. We all have a garden in our lives (such as our families). Like any gardener, we need nourishing ingredients to make our garden grow. If we have more people in our family (or friends in our lives) who are not nourishing, our garden cannot grow. We need to fill our lives with more nourishing people so we can grow.

You are a veritable storehouse, running 24 hours a day, creating thoughts—some of them useful, some of them foolish. And you have a choice out of all of that material that you are creating to choose what you want to use now. Marvelous, isn't it?

We cannot listen to what others want us to do. We must listen to ourselves. Society, family, friends do not know what we must do. Only we know and only we can do what is right for us, so start right now. You will need to work very hard to overcome many obstacles. You'll need to go against the better judgment of many other people. And you will need to bypass their prejudices, but you can have whatever you want if you try hard enough. So, start right now and you'll live a life designed by you and for you and you will love your life.

This is the beginning of a new day. God has given me this day to use it as I will. I can waste it or use it for good. What I do today is important because I'm exchanging a day of my life for it. For tomorrow, this day will be gone forever. Leaving in its place something I have traded for it. I want to gain, not lose. I shall not regret the price I paid for this day.

—Virginia Satir

Seeing the Color of Obama's Heart

I never thought that I, a Jewish woman, would ever be ashamed of some Jewish people who would try to deny a man seeking to become the president of these magnificent United States, because of his color. When will we understand that if we don't start somewhere, there will always be people who don't understand what black people have gone through such horrors ourselves! This young, brilliant Harvard graduate had to be judged as any other young man who believes he can make a difference. I want my young great grandchildren to know I had the chance to help make my beautiful America even better by not seeing the color of a man's skin. I did however see the color of his heart, his warmth, his compassion, his determination, to make the United States the greatest country again.

—From a newspaper column

The Purpose of Life

In some way, however, small and secret, each of us is a little mad. Everyone is lonely at bottom and cries to be understood, but we can never entirely understand someone else. Each of us remains part stranger even to those who love us. It is the weak who are cruel. Gentleness is to be expected only from the strong. Those who do not know fear are not really brave, for courage is the capacity to confront what can be imagined. You can understand people better if you look at them—no matter how old or impressive they may be—as if they are children. For most of us never mature, we simply grow taller. The purpose of life is to matter, to count, to stand for something, to have it make some difference that we lived at all.

—Leo Rosten

Love

Your family can only love you the way they know how. It may never be the way you want love to show up. The greatest gift we can give ourselves is to accept love in all its forms and learn to give ourselves whatever love we did not receive.

Our parents did the best that they could. If they knew a better way, they would have. We must learn to forgive our parents and remember they did the best they could.

—Sid Simon

I believe love when it comes in. It's one of the most profound revelations I've ever heard. Love is all around showing up in small offerings and dramatic encounters and everyday gestures. But we can't receive it if we are fixated on finding it in a package, called parent or husband or love.

—Oprah Winfrey

The happiness you feel is in direct proportion to the love you are able to give. Happiness is never something you get from other people. You lead life; it doesn't lead you. What you are thinking, what you are saying, and what you are doing is having an impact on you and on the people around you right now.

—Oprah Winfrey

Frankly Speaking.

Criticism is an unsolicited opinion from someone else. It is an expression of disapproval either expressed or implied. Beware of sentences that begin with, I am only telling you this for your own good. It is frequently used by others to express their disapproval of you and your actions. Question their motives before you accept it.

Criticism can be based on jealousy. You probably have something they want. The more successful you are, the more criticism you might receive.

Some people cannot bear to have others praised or complimented or held in high esteem.

They feel diminished and insecure. Criticism can come from people who do not understand you or your personal style.

—Patricia C. Frank, *Aventura News.com*, 305-669-7335

Tips on How to Handle Criticism

- Do Not Take It Personally. It is on the opinion of those who are making judgments about you. It does not have to become your internal reality. You do not have to accept their criticism as accurate or as a fact.

- Dismiss It Immediately. Treat it like it is not significant. Ignore insinuations and negative remarks.

- Do Not React or rise to the bait or give any credence to their criticism.

- Control Your Feelings. Put a lid on your feelings and any emotions of anger or resentments you might be feeling.
- Stay Focused on your own thoughts and reality.
- When you start to worry about pleasing someone else, you can become distracted and anxious, which is exhausting emotionally, and you can lose your focus on yourself, who you are and who you want to be.
- Do Not Live to Please. It's Impossible.
- You cannot keep others happy. If they are going to criticize you, they will find a reason to find fault with you. Don't spend your time trying to win your critics over. Not everyone can be excited about your dream thoughts and ideas.
- Do Not Defend Yourself. It puts you in a weakened position and can lead to arguments.
- Keep Your Confidence Up. Get your fire back after the attack.
- Keep Your Heart True. Don't let the criticism change you and make you hard.

—Patricia Frank

Attitude

The longer I live, the more I realize the impact of attitude on life. Attitude, to me, is more important than facts. It is more important than the past, than education, than money, than circumstances, than failures, than successes, than what other people think or say or do. It is more important than appearance, giftedness or skill. It will make or break a company… a church…a home. The remarkable thing is we have a choice every day regarding the attitude we will embrace for that day. We cannot change our past…we cannot change the fact that people will act in a certain way. We cannot change the inevitable. The only thing we can do is play on the one string we have, and that is our attitude…I am convinced that life is 10% what happens to me and 90% how I react to it. And so it is with you…we are in charge of our Attitudes.

—Charles Swindon

Biblical Quotes

The Twenty-Third Psalm

The Lord is My Shepherd;
I Shall not Want.
He has me lie down in Green Pastures.
He leads me beside the Still Waters.
He guides me on Paths of Righteousness,
He revives my Soul for the sake of His Glory.
Though I walk through the valley of the Shadow
 of Death, I fear no harm,
for You are with me.
Your staff and Your rod do comfort me.
You set a table in sight of my enemies;
You anoint my head with oil;
My cup overflows. Surely Goodness
And Mercy shall follow me
all the days of my life, and I shall abide
in the House of the Lord forever.

Proverb 37

A Woman of Valor who can find?
For her price is far above rubies.
The heart of her husband doth safely trust in her,
And he hath no lack of gain.
She doeth him good and not evil
All the days of her life.
Strength and Dignity are her clothing.
And she laughs at the time to come.
She opens her mouth with wisdom;
And kindly counsel is on her tongue.
She looks well to the ways of her household,
And eats not the bread of idleness.
Her children rise up, and call her blessed.
Her husband also, and he praises her:
Many daughters have done valiantly,
But you excel them all.
Grace is deceitful, and beauty is vain.
But a Godfearing woman
She be Praised.
Give her of the fruit of her hands;
And let her own works praise her in the Gates

---

*(*A Woman of Valor *is a very special prayer. My son brought me a framed copy from Israel, and it is so meaningful to me. Traditionally, husbands say this to their wives on Friday evening at the Shabbat table.)*

Jewish Studies

A man should live so that at the close of every day, he can repeat, 'I have not wasted my day.'

—The Zohar

The people worthy of respect are those who give respect, those who hate will be hated. Those who look down on others will be looked down on and those who condemn will be condemned. That is a basic principle of Judaism. In the Old Testament, remember, Do to others that you would have them do to you. This sums up the laws and the prophets. A faithful friend is a powerful defense. He or she that has found such a one has found a treasure.

—Hellenistic Jewish Scribe

If I am not for myself, who will be for me? But if I am only for myself, who am I? And if not now, when?

—Hillel

The study of Torah is our most sacred obligation.

—The Mishnah

Life should be lived as a thank you note to God.

—Rabbi Sugarman of Atlanta

According to Jewish tradition, after a child's Bar or Bat Mitzvah, the role of a mother or father is no longer guilty of their sins. They are going to make their own choices and take the consequences.

The Art of Renewal

Your birthday is the beginning of your own personal new year. Your 1st birthday was a beginning, and each new birthday is a chance to begin again, to start over, to take a new grip on life…

It is a time to toss old hatreds, resentments, grudges and fears into the wastebasket of life; a time to forgive and forget, a time to stretch your soul.

It is a time to list the things you have left undone and to do something about them: the visits you've failed to make, the words unspoken, the letters unwritten, the task unfinished.

It is a time to dust off your dreams and shine up your ideals.

It is a time to browse through the precious old books that have meant the most to you that you may rediscover illuminating phrases and sentences to light your pathway into the future.

It is a time to give thanks to God, and to man, for the riches that have been poured into your life; a time to appreciate anew the beauty and wonder of the world.

The Art of Forgiveness

The art of forgiveness begins when you forgive someone. It is having a humble spirit and being done with pride and self-pity. It is taking a step toward the practice of forgiveness. Hate is death, forgiveness is life. Forgiveness works the miracle of change. When Lincoln was asked why he did not destroy his enemies he replied: If I make my enemies my friends, don't I then destroy them? When you forgive you change others and you change yourself. You change discord to harmony.

Forgiveness should span the years. You should first forgive yourself for the wrongs you've done to yourself and others, for the mistakes you've made. Then you should forgive and bless all those who have wronged you during your lifetime. Thus you release others and you release yourself. You break the chains of regret and remorse that bind you. You free your mind from the burdens of the past so you may walk victoriously into the future.

Forgiveness is the way to personal peace. It is performing mental surgery on yourself, probing deep within to remove hurts, grudges and resentments. It is forgetting wrong as though they had never been. It is flooding your mind with the powerful medicine of forgiveness that cleanses and heals. It is discovering a serenity you've never known before.

One Night I Had a Dream

I dreamed I was walking along the beach with the Lord and across the sky flashed scenes from my life. For each scene I noticed two sets of footprints in the sand. One belonged to me, the other to the Lord.

When the last scene of my life flashed before us, I looked back at the footprints in the sand,

I noticed, that many times along the path of my life, there was only one set of footprints. I also noticed that it happened at the very lowest and saddest times in my life.

This really bothered me, and I questioned the Lord about it. Lord, you said that once I decided to follow you, you would walk with me all the way, but I noticed that during the most troublesome times in my life, there is only one set of footprints. I don't understand why in times when I needed you the most, you would leave me.

The Lord replied, "My precious child, I love you, and I would never, never leave you during your times of trials and suffering. When you see only one set of footprints, it was then that I carried you."

Jewish New Year

The shofar is blown to usher in the Jewish New Year and to serve as a wake-up call for people to reflect on their lives, change their behavior and become better people.

The sound of the shofar resembles a baby's cry. God is the father of all of us and we are his children. We come crying to God at Rosh Hashana to take care of us, to be good to us and bless us with only good things or to bring peace into the world.

If you were to write a leadership book, what would it be called? It would be about teamwork, because that's really what makes everything work. What's so inspiring about being a leader is the energy you get from the group and from seeing how a gem of an idea can grow.

I found this paper that I wrote in 1975 that I used to read at my family's Seders. I asked my son Chayim to read it at his Seder in 2021. I couldn't believe that after more than 45 years the words are still so meaningful, especially at my son's home where all three of his sons are studying to be Rabbis.

> *Tonight, Jews throughout the world will once again gather together with their families and friends to celebrate our freedom from bondage. On this night, which is different from all other nights, let us recall our redemption as free people and rededicate ourselves to the living ties among Jews of all lands. Let us remember the Holocaust survivors. Let us remember our suppressed brethren in Russia and in Arab lands. Let us rededicate ourselves to continuing our support of Israel. Let us welcome the stranger as we remember that we, too, were strangers, and stretch forth our hands to them. Since the Jewish home is considered a miniature sanctuary, it is quite appropriate that it would be modeled along the lines of a Temple. The life which a*

Jew is expected to follow has its roots in the home. It is the training ground for molding character, habits, actions, speech, and thought. The home radiates the teachings of Judaism outside its walls through the example set by those within them.

Rainbow means in Judaism: Teshuva

Noah is the story of one righteous man in an evil generation. He builds an ark on a hill far from water. It took him 120 years. Flood is coming if people don't correct their ways. God brings flood for four days because people do not mend their ways! When one sees a rainbow it is an omen to do teshuva (to recognize the mistakes you are making in life, regret them, correct them, make restitution and ask for forgiveness from anyone you have wronged, as well as the Almighty.) A rabbi asked a student, What have you done with your life? He said married, three sons, and a business. The rabbi says that's not the answer. Have you continued to learn, to grow—to better yourself and this world! That's what is important.

Sukkot

A special commandment for Sukkot is too take the four species etrog, hadassim, lulav, aravot, and wave them in four directions, as well as up and down, meaning God is everywhere. The four species are symbolic of four types of Jews. We bind them together and recognize every Jew as an integral and important part of the Jewish People. Our People are one. We must do all we can to bind together the Jewish people and work to strengthen the Jewish future.

Wisdom from Rabbis

Nine Essential Things I've Learned About Life
by Rabbi Harold Kushner

Harold Kushner has taught a generation of Jews and non-Jews how to understand religion and how to apply its insights to the world in which we live. Now he has written a book that summarizes what he has been teaching all these years in a clear and forthright fashion. Some will be drawn to the chapter that teaches us that God is not a big man in the sky, and that we have to work our way into adulthood before we can understand that. Others will appreciate his chapter on forgiveness, because it teaches that we must forgive, not necessarily because the one who has hurt us deserves it, but because otherwise we will go through life burdened by bitterness that does our enemy no harm and us no good. My favorite chapter in this book is the one that summarizes Harold Kushner's whole theology in one clear and memorable sentence: God does not send the problem; God sends us the strength to deal with the problem.

Clergy Corner by Rabbi Rachel Greengrass,
Temple Beth Am, Miami

While we use the term Jew by choice to describe people who were not born Jewish and who later chose Judaism as their spiritual path—each and every time we pray, study, or do an act of loving kindness, we are choosing Judaism.

We live in a free society, one in which it is frankly easier to choose not to participate in Jewish practice, and yet you (like me) have chosen to be part of the Jewish family. Gone are the days when belonging to a congregation was part of what it meant to be an American, and so your choice is incredibly valuable.

...My grandfather was strawberry blonde and had blue eyes. He spoke perfect Polish and German in addition to the Yiddish he spoke at home and the biblical Hebrew he had mastered as the fifth generation of rabbis in his family. The majority of his family was burned in their synagogue by the Poles, and a few years later, he found himself a slave in the concentration camps. He could've taken on a new identity as a non-Jew. In fact, having run away from the ghetto and then been discovered hiding in a farmer's barn, he was offered the opportunity to marry the farmer's daughter, and have a whole new identity as a Christian. But despite his family being burned alive in their synagogue, despite the horrors of the camps, my grandfather chose to be Jewish.

We choose to be Jewish today. Despite the rise of anti-Semitism, despite the obligations our faith puts on us, despite the fact that there are little to no repercussions for those who walk away from the faith.

We choose Judaism because it gives our lives meaning, because it teaches us how to make the world a better place. Because it gives us the tools to thrive as individuals, and a community where we can raise our children. Because it teaches us how to be *menches* and raise *menches.*

We celebrate the choice our ancestors made back at Mount Sinai; we also celebrate the choice each of us has made, to be Jewish.

Clergy Corner, Rabbi Rachel Greengrass,
Temple Beth Am, Miami

Esther, married to King Ahashverosh and hiding her Judaism, is approached by her Uncle Mordecai, who has discovered that Haman has a plot to wipe out all of the Jewish people. Mordecai tells Esther, "If you remain silent at this time, relief and deliverance for the Jews will rise from another place, but you and your father's family will perish, and who knows maybe you have come to your Royal position for such a time as this."

This line has always spoken to me. I have always tried to live with that idea—perhaps I have been put in my position for a time such as this. It's advice to step up, to do your part. Yet Esther does not lift her head up, shoulders back, and say, "I can do it". No, she says that she can't; she will be killed. And that is how it is for most of us. Life gives us opportunities to step up, and we feel we are not enough, that we might not succeed, so we don't try.

The message Mordecai is giving Esther is: this is your chance, Esther, your chance to fulfill your destiny…to do something great, something you didn't know you were capable of doing.

Each of us has these Esther moments, when we can choose to be the star or remain a background character. Esther was living an inauthentic life, hiding the very soul of who she was. Still, she was comfortable in the palace, a queen. I can think of no more perfect analogy for the American situation today. We are comfortable, yet hiding. So this Purim, let's not only dress up like Esther…let's take this story to heart. There is much work to be done in the world. How can we do our part? Are we willing to risk our perfect comfort for the lives of others or for our own ultimate survival. How are we hiding? How can we use our potential and position to improve the world?

The Road Taken by Rabbi David Wolpe,
Sinai Temple, Los Angeles

What should I do with my life? The question pursues us to the very end of our days. The question of fulfilling our destiny in this world is a constant challenge and provocation.

Some believe each of us should fulfill a fixed, preset design and that life is a search; others believe our purpose is created and that life is a shaping.

Judaism offers both models. There are moments and missions requiring only that we heed the voice: in ancient times, Abraham was chosen and resolute. In modern times, many artists and visionaries felt that they had but to pay attention and their journey was laid clearly before them.

But for the most of us there are multiple paths to walk, as there are multiple partners with whom one might make a life. Each choice will develop unique sides of our characters. The task is not to find the solitary correct road, but to walk one of the roads that will make us better, brighter, more fully realized human beings.

What you are is God's blessings given to you. What you make of yourself is your blessing given to God.

Shabbat Shalom, Rabbi Mark Kram,
Temple Beth Am, Miami, Florida

And so, I take Rabbi Heschel's suggestion as often as I am able to: Lay down the profanity of clattering commerce, of being yoked to toil... go away from the screech of dissonant days, from the nervousness and fury of acquisitiveness and the betrayal in embezzling our own lives... to understand that the world has already been created and will survive without my help. Six days a week we wrestle with the world, wringing profit from the earth; on the Sabbath we especially care for the seed of eternity planted in the soul. Six days a week we seek to dominate the world, on the seventh day, we try to dominate the self.

The meaning of the Sabbath is to celebrate time rather than space. Six days a week we live under the tyranny of things of space; on the Sabbath we try to become attuned to holiness in time. It is a day on which we are called upon to share in what is eternal in time, to turn from the results of creation to the mystery of creation; from the world of creation to the creation of the world. I encourage you to do the same.

Ethical Wills, Rabbi Mark Kram,
Temple Beth Am, Miami, Florida

When we finally leave this earth, what do we leave behind? What do we leave our children or grandchildren to remember us by? If we're smart, we leave a will, a plan for our estate. The legal will serves a limited purpose. Something is missing…what's happens to our ethical values after death?… A wonderful old Jewish custom is to sum up in a letter all a parent had learned in life—and to express what they wanted most for their children. What a meaningful gift to give to those who remain. One writer called an ethical will "a legacy of intangibles."

What bits of wisdom learned in life would we like to impart? What precious advice would we give? Three messages are apparent: money is not the most important thing; remain Jews; stay close to each other. Hear my values and follow them. The values we live for, the good things for which we worked or stood for, are more important than those physical things we may leave behind.

Being able to commit into writing my deepest feelings about life through an ethical will for my children is comforting. Explaining my priorities and my purpose, the things that truly matter, allows me to put into writing before I die, what I wish for them. I will rest a bit easier because I know that even if unspoken during my lifetime, my feelings will be known. Maybe with luck, my children will come to share the same priorities.

Those who write ethical wills assure that their values as well as their property will last after they are gone. They are written by people who understand that you and I are not completely dead when we die if we leave behind people who understand what we stood for and who will carry on what we believed in.

Love Your Neighbor, by Rabbi Zelig Pliskin

A person who finds fault with inanimate objects (food, accommodations, etc.) will also find fault with people. Conversely, a person who always seeks to find the good in things will also see the good in his fellow man.

Rabbi Avi Weiss

A grandparent's relationship to a child, on some level, is deeper than a parent/child relationship. Unencumbered by parental responsibility, a grandparent, blessed with wisdom and maturity of life, can powerfully bestow blessings on their grandchildren. In a brief instant, a grandparent asks, mi eileh? who are these?, not so much as a question, but as an expression of thanks to God for having been blessed with glorious grandchildren.

Rabbi Terry A. Bookman, *Temple Beth Am, Miami, Florida*

For most of us, Chanukkah has become a time of gift giving and receiving and decorating our homes. There is nothing wrong with this. I love to give gifts and sense the joy that brings to the lives of others. But if that is all our Chanukkah is about, then we miss its true import.

The real symbol of Chanukkah is the menorah. During these eight days we will light the menorah in our homes, adding one candle for each night. Just when the days are at their shortest, we Jews bring light to our often fragmented and broken world. It is our response to the pain and adversity which we see and feel in those around us. To light a candle is a symbol of faith and hope, an act of defiance. It says, we will not be defeated; rather, we will live on. It is a little thing, but here we are, some two thousand years later, still lighting the world with our special light.

But that is not all we can do. We can lessen the pain and adversity others face—the hungry and the homeless, the sick and the infirmed, the impoverished and the elderly, the lonely and the lost at heart. We do not need to go far to seek them. They are all around us. They may be our friends and neighbors, members of our family, even ourselves. We need to see them all with our hearts. In the end, perhaps this Chanukkah can inspire us to flavor our world with more love and kindness.

The Garden of Gratitude, by Rabbi Shalom Arush

The Torah relates The man Moses was the most humble of men. Gratitude is a character trait that stems from humility. When a person sees how good Hashem is to him, and how much he gives him, he becomes more humble and thinks: Me? *Who am I? Do I deserve all that Hashem gives me?* He even feels embarrassed and grows that much more humble.

...One who invests time and effort in striving to be a grateful person will ultimately attain humility, which in turn will help him defeat his evil inclination. Therefore strengthening gratitude has a direct, positive effect on improving one's mood!

A person with a morsel of integrity admits the obvious: he deserves nothing. He relies only on the Mercy of God. Truth and humility go together, for as soon as a person casts his arrogance aside, he realizes what are we, what are our lives worth, what is our righteousness, what is our strength, what is our bravery?

Gratitude guards us against taking our many blessings for granted! In this way, faith and gratitude purify and uplifts our hearts (that's how I feel when I help others).

Our Jewish Heritage, Rabban Simeon Ben Gamaliel

The world stands on three things: *on Torah, on worship, and on deeds of loving kindness*. The word Torah is not just the physical Torah. It represents all sources of Jewish learning. The word Worship, it represents prayer worship. Participating in a prayer service is a way to bring us closer to God and the community. The third word, Deeds of Loving Kindness, urges us to participate in daily actions that help others. When we perform these acts of kindness, we display the godliness within each of us!

He also says: The World is sustained by three things, by Justice, by Truth, by Peace. The opposites are injustice, lies, violence, and war. There can be no Justice, if there is no Truth. There can be no peace between people and communities, if there is an atmosphere of injustice, lies, and violence. Jewish tradition and American tradition blend together on what is essential to bring peace within our cities and borders. These values guide us to strive to improve Ourselves, Our Community, and Our Country.

A Lifelong Love Affair with God, Rabbi Rami Shapiro

By conscious practice, I simply mean that we pay attention to our thoughts, words, and deeds, and do our best to see that our behavior honors the other as well as the self, knowing that both are manifestations of God. Spirituality is about what you do, not what you think or how you feel. We don't become conscious. We live consciously. When we talk about becoming conscious, we make things very mysterious. I don't think there is any mystery in spirituality at all. There is awareness and there is delusion. There is kindness and there is exploitation. Where is the mystery? As for their virtues the spiritual person cultivates, these are universal: justice, compassion, honesty, humility, and the like. We make spirituality mysterious and complicated so as to excuse ourselves from being kind, compassionate, honest, and just. Life is really quite simple. You are born, you live, and you die. You act kindly or cruelly; you are generous or stingy; you are loving or fearful. No mystery here. You want mystery, invent theology, past lives, heavens, and hells. But this is only in your mind. There is no mystery, only reality. You need to live with attention or not.

***Minyan & Prayer,** Rebel Goldberg Bader*

While I was rewriting my short story, "Praying," a close friend suddenly and unexpectedly died. The idea of healing both the dead and the living through prayer came to me while writing this story. I wanted to be part of creating a healing space. The Minyan provides that space and becomes a place where one can confront grief, find support, and begin the healing process. After my friend's death, I felt that, in spite of the early hour and the long drive to the synagogue, I wanted to be counted among the ten individuals necessary to assure the Minyan. The Minyan proved to be a gift. Through this one hour, whether I was called up to the Torah to pray or if I took part in any of the devotional blessings, just by being there, I had been healed, embraced by holiness, and gathered up in awe.

Oprah Winfrey once asked: If you had one gift to give the world, what would it be and why? Or, what dream is yet to be realized for you? I answered her question this way:

"I know what my dream would be right now. Before I die, our family can be together, my children, grandchildren and great-grandchildren in the same room!"

That's what I'm working toward for my 90th birthday party and book-signing celebration on June 20, 2021, at the Vi of Aventura, Florida, where I live now.

Acknowledgments

I want to thank…

My family—My three children, my seven grandchildren, and my six great-grandchildren are all included in my autobiography with pictures. I am forever grateful for my family and the ones who are yet to come.

My new friends at the Vi for all their love and support, including Betty, Dorothy and Heather and, of course, Rachel Lapidot, who created my invitation and taught me to enter the new age of technology with my new iPhone. I also dearly remember my Vi friends who have passed on.

Rabbi Menachem Smith, who teaches a weekly Torah class at the Vi of Aventura where I have lived for the past five years. It is so important to study Torah. His Torah lessons at the Vi have enabled me to continue my learning.

William LaPato, Vice President of Merrill Lynch in Boca, who is my financial advisor and has given me peace of mind. He figured out how I could move here and enjoy my life now. He has kept me living for the past 15 years. I am grateful for his wisdom and honesty.

My wonderful, talented, and patient book designer and production manager, Gary Rosenberg of The Book Couple in Boca Raton.

My editor, Erica Rauzin. I am eternally grateful for what she has helped me accomplish. I sorted material I collected for more than 40 years of studies and gave Erica the job of putting it on paper. She was able to extract the essence of my emotional growth through the teachers' material I supplied. The finished product is more than I ever dreamed possible.

I hope this book will enable my family and friends and those who will read it to grow emotionally and spiritually.

www.ingramcontent.com/pod-product-compliance
Ingram Content Group UK Ltd.
Pitfield, Milton Keynes, MK11 3LW, UK
UKHW062312290726
14090UKWH00018B/1023